The Real

THE REAL BATTLE

Ray Beeson

Tyndale House Publishers
Wheaton, Illinois

ACKNOWLEDGMENTS

To Carol Lacy and Carol Patterson whose valuable assistance in editing have made this book possible. Their knowledge and abilities as well as their gentleness of spirit have been of tremendous encouragement to me.

To Joyce Howell who devoted so much time to typing the original draft.

To pastors Lance Ralston and Dave Guzik who spent many hours with me poring over this work. Their labor of love has added to this work significantly and to my life tremendously.

To Dr. Bob Fortin and his wife Jeannie whose lives have blessed mine so very much.

The unselfish efforts of these people on behalf of others bear great testimony to the presence of Jesus Christ in their lives. I am forever grateful for their love.

For information on Ray Beeson's ministry of training Christians in effective spiritual warfare and prayer write: Overcomers Ministries, 7357 Wolverine St., Ventura, CA 93003.

Material from *Prayer is Invading the Impossible,* by Jack Hayford (copyright 1977) is reprinted by permission of Bridge Publishing, South Plainfield, NJ 07080.

Scripture quotations are from *The Holy Bible,* New International Version (NIV), copyright 1978 by Zondervan Publishing House, Grand Rapids, Michigan, unless otherwise indicated as being from: *The Living Bible* (TLB), copyright 1971 by Tyndale House Publishers, Wheaton, Illinois; *The Holy Bible,* New King James Version (NKJV), copyright 1979, 1980, 1982 by Thomas Nelson, Inc., Nashville, Tennessee; *The Holy Bible,* King James Version (KJV).

To the most wonderful person I have ever met,
my wife Linda

CONTENTS

FOREWORD

S. D. Gordon once said, "To adequately define prayer, one must use the language of war." The noted author and preacher explained, "Peace language is not equal to the situation. The earth is in a state of war and is being hotly beseiged. Thus, one must use war talk to grasp the fact with which prayer is concerned. Prayer from God's side is communication between himself and his allies in the enemy country."

In *Destined for the Throne,* Dr. Billheimer expands this idea: "The prayer closet is the *arena* which produces the overcomer. The world is a laboratory in which those destined for the throne are learning in actual practice how to overcome Satan and his hierarchy. This means that redeemed humanity outranks all other orders of created beings in the universe."

With keen insight concerning prayer's power, Billheimer goes on to say that "the church, through her resurrection and ascension with Christ, is already legally on the throne. Through this use of her weapons of prayer and faith, she holds in this present throbbing moment the balance of power in the world affairs. In spite of all her lamentable weaknesses, appalling failures, and indefensible shortcomings, the Church is the mightiest force for civilization and enlightened social consciousness in the world today."

The real battle, as Ray Beeson so aptly explains in this much-needed manual on spiritual warfare, is in the invisible heavenlies. Until we recognize the significance of this reality and apply the biblical principles that equip us for the conflict, any hope of lasting spiritual victory is all but impossible. Our weapons, after all, are "not the weapons of the world," but those which have "divine power to demolish strongholds" (2 Cor. 10:4, NIV).

In *The Real Battle*, Ray Beeson not only defines this conflict but also paints a practical picture for understanding this warfare and for engaging in it with an absolute assurance of victory. I commend these pages to you with the prayer that you will find them as challenging and as helpful as did this pilgrim of prayer.

> Dick Eastman
> *Executive Director*
> *Change the World Ministries*

PREFACE

Several years ago, while working in the "Change the World School of Prayer" department at World Literature Crusade, I traveled thousands of miles across America teaching on the subject of prayer. God's Spirit worked wonderfully through the ministry. But the more he worked, the more I became aware of the spiritual battle going on about us: a battle between those who love the Lord and the "rulers . . . authorities . . . the powers of this dark world and . . . the spiritual forces of evil in the heavenly realms" (Eph. 6:12).

It seemed there was a struggle against this unseen enemy on nearly every front. Trying to figure it all out wasn't easy and questions were abundant. Why did there seem to be one battle right after another? Why didn't God rescue those of us who were facing problems? Why did he allow so many heartaches? Why, God? Why such a struggle? I knew in my spirit that "the one who is in [me] is greater than the one who is in the world" (1 John 4:4), but something was amiss concerning the release of God's power—and I couldn't figure out what it was.

Most of us who want to please the Lord eventually come to a place where theology and reality appear to clash head-on. The problem then is to put the pieces together. This book came from my search for answers to some tough questions in three of the greatest and most difficult subjects in Christian theology: 1) the origin of Satan, 2) the origin of sin, and 3) the makeup of man.

I am not a theologian. As a scholar I fall far short of the qualifications to do justice to these three important topics. But because of some experiences in face-to-face conflict with the strongholds of Satan, I have sought to find what God's Word teaches on these subjects. And now I want to share my findings with those of you who also feel the intensity of the battle.

An exhaustive study of any one of these subjects would require volumes. The attempt to put them together in one volume may not be as scholarly as some would either like or require. But what I hope it will do is alert many to the fact that there is more that we as Christians must deal with than just the "cares of this life." As someone has said, "Your greatest spiritual attack won't be a flat tire on the freeway." There's a war going on!

Within the text you will find a variety of insights from respected Christians who also have sought answers to questions about the unseen. I trust their insights will bless you as they have blessed me.

Satan is real! If you haven't already discovered this, just commit yourself to becoming a prayer warrior, a soul winner, or to any part of the kingdom of God that requires the power and presence of the Holy Spirit beyond God's saving grace.

In order for us to live as God desires and to be overcomers, it is important that we understand a number of things. One of those things is the inception of sin. When we understand what is wrong with us, it is much easier to follow biblical directives to see things made right. The way God has made us, the way in which the enemy works, the weapons we have available to us, and the authority we have in Christ all are things we must understand to fight effectively in the war at hand.

To better understand how that war affects each of us personally, I've tried to explain many problems through describing the body, soul, and spirit. I realize knowledge in these areas is quite limited and that there is much controversy as to how these parts of humanity actually exist. I don't profess to be an expert on these elements, but I have found many answers by studying them. And I have found that God created us in a far more complex manner than anyone can explain. I only hope you will find this book to be a help and a blessing as you seek to increase your understanding.

One last thought: Balance in anything is never easy. As necessary as it is, balance can be rather evasive at times. In writing a book on the devil there is always the danger of missing or forgetting some important truth, especially a truth that emphasizes the power of God. As you read, please keep in mind the sovereignty of God and his ability to guide and keep those who are his. It may be a good idea for you to read Psalm 135 before you begin, for this Psalm acknowledges God's authority.

As you look at the struggle, you may be tempted to throw up your hands and quit. That is exactly what the enemy wants. But if you want God, he wants you and will prove himself powerful to you as you continue to seek him.

I pray this book will give you some practical guidelines for fighting in a very real spiritual war.

AN OVERVIEW

Some years ago a short, squat, little character, who looked more like an upright turtle without his shell than an intelligent creature from outer space, came to the movie screen. He was called the Extra-Terrestrial—"E.T." for short. Kids, parents, and grandparents alike adored him. He created a renewed hope that there might be someone beyond our sphere of intelligence, strength, and understanding who knows what is going on and who could deliver us from the tangled messes in which we find ourselves. And, despite the fact that he was merely a substitute, he rekindled once again our inherent desire for a savior.

Well, I have good news! The whole scenario is not as fantastic as it may seem. Someone *did* come from another world to planet earth. He was an extra-terrestrial in the fullest sense of the word. He was an "outsider," an "invader."

News of his coming started quietly, almost unnoticed: "He is coming," said a prophet. "He will rescue us when he comes," said another. And another, and another. And hope began to arise. "Hold on, help is on the way." But centuries passed and he didn't come.

As he waited, man's mind probably did not remain idle. Many probably began to imagine what would happen when the "Savior" finally did come. "Sudden and powerful must his entry be." "Sword against sword our King will appear to take vengeance upon our enemies." "Our Creator will send his Anointed One and we will be free. Free at last!"

And so men continued to await the promised Messiah. But as is always the case, the struggle of life soon wrested away their awareness and expectancy of this prophesied event until, for many, hope probably was relegated to the ethereal. "It may happen," the mind said quietly, "but not where I'm standing." The cares of life so occupied men's minds that only during a crisis did they hope for something better and direct their attention for a brief moment toward the promised redemption.

Then, with very little fanfare, the true Messiah descended on earth. Not with conquering sword and spear, horse and chariot, and shout of triumph—but rather with the sound of a baby's cry. No conqueror had ever burst forth into the arena of battle with the squeal of an infant. Could this really be the promised one?

But while mankind was puzzling over the "good news of great joy" (Luke 2:10), the demons "in the heavenly realm" trembled. Suddenly, for the first time since the man Adam, there was a person over whom the enemy of man's soul had no control. Satan's hordes scurried to understand the significance of God incarnate—deity in human flesh.

And eventually mankind, too, struggled to understand the meaning of this event: Why didn't God send an entire invasion force? Why only an infant? Why didn't he just come and do away with sin and suffering and death instantly?

God did not do these things because he would not violate mankind's free will. He refused to arbitrarily step in and solve our problems; we would have to cooperate in the rescue effort. But that was impossible since we were in slavery to Satan. Without God we were powerless to break away from our bondage to the enemy and to sin. So, in God's beautiful plan of redemption, he became a man himself. A sinless man. There would be no sinful nature in him to bring him into bondage—he was the first man since Adam who was without sin and thus totally free from Satan's domination. And he came to rescue us. He came to break the power of sin and Satan.

Here was a man who could rightfully reclaim the

earth that mankind lost through disobedience. As Adam had power over Satan before the fall because he was sinless, now this second sinless Adam would have power over the enemy.

However, stopping Satan's power against humanity required mighty action: the world had to be redeemed, bought back. And the only price that was adequate was the *death* of this second Adam. For it was the sacrificial death of this child, when he reached manhood, that would pronounce doom on the entire realm of rebellious angels. The price of Jesus' blood was the only thing that could release us from sin and separation from God on the one hand and from slavery to Satan on the other. So die he did. But he didn't stay dead: "God raised him from the dead, . . . because it was impossible for death to keep its hold on him" (Acts 2:24).

Through this Savior the powers of Satan were broken and he was defeated. Yet, although Satan and his cohorts were judged and found guilty, their sentences would not be carried out immediately. And in the meantime we would learn to cooperate in our own deliverance. It was true there was nothing we could do to pay for our salvation. But we *could* participate in our own deliverance by yielding ourselves to our new King, by learning to fight in a war taking place on the spiritual plane—a war in which we would help bring to pass the sentences of those the King of kings has reserved for judgment because of their wickedness.

And so the war continues to rage. Though we once were so bound we couldn't fight, now the Captain of our salvation is here to secure our release and lead us into battle. And in the pages that follow, you will discover your position in that very real, ongoing war.

ONE

Understanding
the Unseen

In his book *Providential Deliverances,* W. A. Spicer describes the experience of a man named Hokland who was a missionary in Norway. Because he wanted to reach families living in a hidden valley, Hokland had to descend a treacherous mountain trail. At one steep, dangerous place he stopped to pray, asking God to send his angel to go with him. Soon he reached the valley safely.

He approached the first cottage where he met a man and his wife who had been watching his descent of the dangerous trail.

"What has become of your companion?" was their first question after the usual greeting.

"What companion?" asked the missionary.

"The man who was with you."

"But there was no one with me; I am traveling alone."

"Is that possible?" they exclaimed in surprise. "We were watching you as you came down the mountain and it seemed to us there were two men crossing the mountain together."

"[It was] then," reported missionary Hokland, "that I

was reminded of my prayer to God for help, and of the word of the Lord in Psalm 34:7, 'The angel of the Lord encampeth round about them that fear him and delivereth them.' "[1] This man's experience is similar to thousands of other miraculous events described by missionaries and other Christian workers for years. In this chapter, we will discuss the spiritual world where God's angels—as well as demon spirits—exist; a realm seldom seen by natural eyes. We will learn that we must become familiar with all the forces and powers in this unseen dimension in order to fight effectively in the battle around us.

GOD'S SPIRITUAL FORCES

Elisha the prophet was once an adviser to the king of Israel. When Israel was at war with the king of Syria, God told Elisha of the enemy king's plans, and Elisha sent word of those plans to the king of Israel. Israel's enemy, the king of Syria, became greatly frustrated because of continual defeat, so he "summoned his officers and demanded of them, 'Will you not tell me which of us is on the side of the king of Israel?' " (2 Kings 6:11). One of the officers assured the king that none of his men were spies, but that Israel had Elisha the prophet telling the Israelite king the very words the Syrian king spoke in his bedroom.

When the Syrian king discovered Elisha was in Dothan, he sent horses, chariots, and a great army by night and surrounded the entire town. The next morning when Elisha's servant arose and looked out, he was struck with fear at the sight of such a great host. "Oh, my lord," he said, "what shall we do?" The prophet responded by saying, "Do not be afraid. . . . Those who are with us are more than those who are with them" (2 Kings 6:15-16).

"Surely you're joking," the servant must have thought. "We have nowhere near the men for battle that they have."

Have you ever been in a situation where you could not see past what your natural eyes revealed? That's what happened with this poor servant. All he knew was that there was a great enemy army before them and the smell of death all around, and so he succumbed to the fear generated by natural sight.

Elisha, on the other hand, looked past the natural and into the realm of the spiritual, where by faith he beheld God's mighty host ready for battle. All around them he saw an army of angelic soldiers that far outnumbered the Syrians—a very real and powerful army. What a sight that must have been! Then Elisha prayed and his servant's eyes were opened so that he too could see that the hills were full of horses and chariots of fire of the Lord. And he realized God had sent his powerful angelic army to rescue them.

This is only one Old Testament account of battles fought in the presence of, or with the help of, angels. In addition to Elisha at Dothan (2 Kings 6), we can read about God's angels, who were the instruments of destruction in Sodom and Gomorrah (Gen. 19:12-13); Michael and a messenger angel in Persia (Dan. 10); and the angel of the Lord with Gideon (Judg. 6). In Revelation we read that Michael and his angels will fight Satan and his angels (Rev. 12) and that it is an angel who will place Satan in the bottomless pit (Rev. 20:1-3).

When Jesus was accosted in the Garden of Gethsemane, Peter went to his defense with a sword. But Jesus told him, "Do you think I cannot call on my Father, and he will at once put at my disposal more than twelve legions of angels?" (Matt. 26:53). Here was a powerful spiritual population ready for battle if

Christ should call. It may be difficult to comprehend, but God's mighty host of angels is still all around us (Heb. 12:22; 13:2).

Jesus also encountered the spiritual forces of the demon realm. (The word *demon,* although not used in the King James Version of Scripture, is used today to denote evil spirits.) During his temptation in the wilderness, the devil took him up into a "high mountain and showed him all the kingdoms of the world and their splendor" (Matt. 4:8). What was Jesus looking at? Was it a vision of all the nations and individual cities of the earth? Or was he really looking at the nucleus of spiritual power under Satan's control, the most powerful of the demons—those next to Satan himself? Was he seeing the core of Satan's "rulers . . . authorities . . . powers of this dark world and . . . spiritual forces of evil in the heavenly realms" (Eph. 6:12)?

Was Jesus seeing the very real kingdom of spirit beings who operate behind the scenes, most often undetected by natural man? Isn't it possible that Satan was telling Jesus that if he would fall down and worship him, hordes of demon powers would come under his control and he would become second in command?

Jesus knew enough of Satan's schemes to take him seriously. He responded, "Away from me, Satan! For it is written: 'Worship the Lord your God, and serve him only' " (Matt. 4:10). And we need to take Satan seriously too. But to do so, we need to understand where Satan found his army of spiritual beings or demons.

THE DEMON REALM

Satan's host is comprised of angels who have fallen away from or rebelled against God (2 Pet. 2:4; Jude 6; Rev. 12:4).[2] They are typically referred to as demons, devils, or evil spirits. These evil beings maintain a conscious state of existence, are hostile to God, and are disposed to lead us against him. They are not some figment of our imaginations, an error of our minds, an abstract power, a concept, or a way of explaining the evil found in the human heart. Neither are they little creatures—complete with horns, sharp tails, and hooves—who run around in red suits and carry pitchforks.

These spiritual beings have caused much of the chaos in the world around us and much of the disintegration of our present society. The fallen condition of the human heart is not the only explanation for the terrible things that happen every day. The extent and intensity of the depravity and wickedness of mankind, and the corruption of our current world system, can be accounted for only by a host of unseen evil spirits who are working to accomplish Satan's wishes for our destruction. To try to understand and deal with the many problems of the human race without acknowledging this army of fiendish spiritual beings leaves us far short of providing a solution for the difficulties and trials we face.

Created somewhat different than mankind (Ps. 8:5; Heb. 2:7), these fallen, rebellious angels chose to break rank with God and follow another very powerful, yet created, angel into anarchy. During the initial rebellion they were organized into a hierarchy. The biblical terms "rulers," "authorities," "the powers of this dark world," and "spiritual forces of evil in the heavenly realms" (Eph. 6:12) all refer to a well-organized army. A scriptural study of their nature shows that they possess knowledge and intelligence (Matt. 8:29; Luke 4:41; Acts 16:16-17; 19:15); that they are powerful (Mark 5:1-20; 2 Thess. 2:9; Rev. 16:13-14); that they are individuals (Mark 16:9); that they teach doctrines (1 Tim. 4:1); and that they do not possess their own

[handwritten margin note: Description of what we're up against.]

21

natural or spirit bodies, yet desire to do so (Mark 5:12; Acts 16:16-18; Rev. 16:13-14).

The chief among the demons is most often called Satan, but his original name was Lucifer.[3] Although to some his name may inspire negative connotations, *Lucifer* originally was a beautiful name basically meaning "Light Bearer" or "Shining One." When this prince among the angels rebelled and persuaded myriad other angels to follow him, his name was changed. In Scripture, names often reflect character traits; thus, when Lucifer's character changed, God changed his name to reflect his new character. His new name, *Satan*, means "adversary."

In the introduction to his book *Satan*, Lewis Sperry Chafer comments:

> Without reference to revelation, the world has imagined a grotesque being, fitted with strange trappings, who has been made the central character in works of fiction and theatrical performances, and by this relation to that which is unreal, the character of Satan has come to be considered only one of the myths of a bygone age.
>
> The Bible reveals a detailed description of the person and career of Satan beginning with creation, and includes his original condition, his fall, the development and manifestation of his kingdom, and his final defeat and banishment. It presents a personage so mighty and so prominent in the world today that the Christian heart would fail, were it not for faith in the One who has triumphed over all principalities and powers.[4]

Who Is This Satan? Ezekiel 28 describes Satan in a "double reference." It appears that God, through Ezekiel, is speaking to the king of Tyre, but a careful examination shows that God is also speaking to the spiritual being controlling this wicked king. In verses 14 and 16, the spirit is referred to as a cherub; in this case, a rebellious or fallen cherub (angel). Verses 13 and 15 refer to this spirit as a created being. And what a creation he was initially! He was perfect, full of wisdom, and beautiful (v. 12); he had been in the Garden of Eden (v. 13); he was an anointed guardian angel, and originally he was blameless (v. 14). He held an extremely high position before God, but a day came when unrighteousness was found in him.

How could such an exalted creation with all of his honor fall away from God? What would cause him to do such a thing? The answer is that God gave him a free will just as he gave to all other similar created beings. So Satan had the power to choose, which provided him with the opportunity to rebel.

Both men and angels have been given the power of choice to keep them from being little more than robots or puppets. God, with his tremendous love, wants his creation to submit to him not by force but from heartfelt desire and love. For love is not really love if we are forced into it.

Satan's rebellion was not due to any inequities on God's part. In fact, God cannot be blamed for evil nor can it even be said that he in any way created it.[5] God simply created an orderly universe of beings who had free will and who were expected to operate within an established framework. And some, using their free will, have chosen to rebel.

Satan's demons continuously shove in our faces the idea that we should make God responsible for sin and evil: "If he created everything, then obviously he created error." But Satan's sinful rebellion was due entirely to his own deception. He became lifted up with pride because of his beauty and prominence, and then, thinking himself to be as good as God, he tried to be like him. Ezekiel 28:16 could indicate that Satan's unrighteousness was sealed by peer pressure. "Through your *widespread trade* you were filled with violence, and you sinned" (italics added). Lucifer perhaps slandered God until he had an audience. Then his hearers began to prod him to do something, and soon the rebellion was in full swing.

It is important to keep in mind that Satan is a real, created person (not a human, but an individual with personality nonetheless) with thoughts, feelings, and desires (Isa. 14:12-16; Matt. 8:29; 12:43-45; Mark 5:7; Acts 8:7). He is described in Scripture as a deceiver, a liar, a thief, a murderer, the god of this age, and the ruler of this world. He is also likened to a roaring lion, a serpent, and a dragon.

If he is regarded as an imaginary being, it is obviously impossible to deal with him. In Scripture we are told to resist and to fight against him. Such admonition would be pointless if he did not exist.

However, although he is a powerful leader of fallen angels and rebellious men, Satan is not omnipotent. And though it is true that his influence is widespread, he is not omnipresent. He may have tremendous knowledge, but he is not omniscient.

Chafer says further, "Since he was created, he is not self-existent, and never can be free from his dependence upon the Creator. He may vainly propose to become independent, and even be permitted for a time to act under that delusion; but that only delays the inevitable judgment that awaits him. He was created perfect, or was a perfect fulfillment of the Creator's intention. Satan was a free moral agent, capable of choosing evil but not obliged to do so. That he chose evil must ever be to his own condemnation, for the Creator had surrounded him with sufficient motives for choosing the good."[6]

What Is Satan Trying to Accomplish? The book of Isaiah helps us understand some of Satan's purposes and goals. What appears in this prophet's writings to be God's judgment on Babylon and its king is also a judgment on the enemy himself. Babylon was so given to demon influence that the two, the city itself and demons, could not be separated. What God would do to one, he would do to the other.

Isaiah 14 records five things Satan wanted to accomplish. They are his five "I will's." He says first, "I will ascend to heaven." God gave him a dominion outside of heaven, a place he could govern. Some consider this place to be earth before Adam's time. But the location of this place is not as important as the fact that wherever Satan was coming from he was now journeying back to heaven with war in mind. This we see from his next statement where he says, "I will raise my throne above the stars of God" (v. 13). Here he establishes an aspiration for power and position that were not rightfully his.

Then he says, "I will sit enthroned on the mount of assembly, on the utmost heights of the sacred mountain" (v. 13). There is a strong possibility that the "mount of assembly" is where formal praise to God takes place. It is, possibly, the place where angels wonderfully and gloriously worship God. Satan no doubt wanted to be praised. He desired the same admiration he saw God receiving in the attention his angels gave him, attention that came out of God's love relationship with the angels.

Fourth, he says, "I will ascend above the tops of the clouds" (v. 14), and finally, "I will make myself like the Most High" (v. 14). It is in this, his last statement, that we see his ultimate goal: to be a god, similar to the one and only true God.

Ethel Barrett, in her beautiful allegory *The Great Conflict*, writes:

The problem was Lucifer.
Lucifer, not content with what he had, wanted to be as powerful as Shaddai himself, and persuaded the

angels to rebel, and the place in the Universe where this rebellion was perpetrated was called Earth, and Lucifer was confident that the rebellion would be successful.[7]

Again Chafer comments:

There could be but one Most High, and the purpose of Satan to become like Him could, naturally, be nothing less than an attempt to dethrone the Almighty. . . .The secret purpose in his heart reveals his method to be not a violent attack upon the throne, but, like Absalom, to steal the hearts of the unfaithful in the kingdom, and, through subtlety, to gain a kingdom for himself. He would thus become an object of worship and attract attention from other beings to himself.[8]

After "stealing the hearts of the unfaithful," Satan evidently became so arrogant he actually believed he could conquer heaven. It must have been a quick battle, for Jesus says, "I saw Satan fall like lightning from heaven" (Luke 10:18; Ezek. 28:16). Notice that Jesus did not say that he had cast him out. Nor did he indicate involvement on the part of the Father or the Holy Spirit. He only said that he saw it happen. From the Book of Revelation we conclude that it was, no doubt, Michael and other nonrebellious angels with him who fought Satan and his demon angels. And it appears that Satan will make a last attempt to conquer heaven at a future time, and Michael and his host will again rout the enemy and cast him back down to earth (Rev. 12:7-9).

Satan's Power Is Not God's Power. Satan's desire was to be "like God." For all practical purposes, he has accomplished that goal in the eyes of much of the world and, believe it or not, in the eyes of many Christians. Let's play a little game to prove this point. It is called the

Antonym Game. Antonyms, of course, are words of opposite meaning. Here are some questions. You respond:

What is the opposite of up?

"Simple," you say, "down."

What is the opposite of backward?

"Simple again, forward."

What is the opposite of left?

"Easy, it's right."

What is the opposite of God?

"That's easy also, it's Satan."

That is what most people assume. And that is exactly what Satan wants. The popular Christian theologian, C. S. Lewis, clarifies it in this way:

> The commonest question is whether I really "believe in the Devil." Now, if by "the Devil" you mean a power opposite to God and, like God, self-existent from all eternity, the answer is certainly No. There is no uncreated being except God. God has no opposite. No being could attain a "perfect badness" opposite to the perfect goodness of God; for when you have taken away every good thing (intelligence, will, memory, energy, and existence itself) there would be none of him left.[9]

Opposites have a degree of similarity in that in their association they become "like" one another. Satan chose to try to be God's opposite in order to be like him. So far he has succeeded quite well. But we must remember that God is eternal, Satan is created. There is no one like God, so there is no one equally his opposite. Praise God for the assurance this gives as we examine Satan's characteristics. Satan cannot possibly, at any time, ever overcome God! On that basis, then, such a study need not be approached with fear. Simply put, there is no antonym *or* synonym for God. "For who in the skies above can compare with the Lord? Who is like the Lord among the heavenly beings?" (Ps. 89:6-7).

If you would like an antonym for Satan, try Michael, who is another created being in league with God and who has fought with Satan on different occasions (Dan. 10:13; Jude 9; Rev. 12:7).

SATAN, THE PRINCE OF THIS WORLD

Scripture makes it clear that Satan is the prince of this world: "I will not speak with you much longer, for the prince of this world is coming," Jesus said (John 14:30; 12:31; 16:11).

Many people, including Christians, believe that God is in control of earth in such a way that he causes everything to happen—both the good and the evil. Now most, it is true, do not believe that he creates evil. But they do believe he allows it, which often translates into almost the same as if he actually created it. To say that he is not in control or at least not presently controlling is to some an infringement upon his sovereignty. It is true that the physical planet is the Lord's (Exod. 9:39; Ps. 24:1). But we must remember that initially it was leased to mankind; it was given to him to control. Now, because much of the control of the earth is in the hands of those who belong to Satan, he has much of the control of earth. The condition of the human heart determines whether God or Satan rules the person and thus the earth. For now, God has chosen to control only the places we will yield to him.

When we resist the enemy and turn to righteousness through Christ, God permits his Holy Spirit to set up a bastion for protection within the human heart, as well as a beachhead for continued operations. These fortifications and operations in the hearts of millions of believers worldwide are keeping Satan from total control of earth. So, even though God by his own choice is not in control of all that happens on earth at present, he can guide and protect us if we submit to him. Make no mistake, the purposes of Satan and other rebellious offenders will come to an end. God has not lost control of earth as if someone more powerful wrestled it from him. He is still completely sovereign. God does not forcibly exert control because he won't override free will. And he continues to allow the present distress in order to prove the utter fallacy of sin and rebellion. But a day will come when the purposes of God will be revealed and he will exercise total control.

Satan is further referred to as the "Prince of the power of the air" (Eph. 2:2), indicating his powerful spiritual realm here on earth. Note that the spiritual realm controls the natural realm. The natural realm is subject to both natural and spiritual law. By directing one (the spiritual) and influencing the other (the natural), Satan now controls both areas. Until we allow Jesus Christ entrance into our lives we are subject to Satan's control. Through Christ we can be free from the enemy's grasp. But we must make the choice as to whom we will serve.

The period of time between Christ's death and Satan's defeat at Armageddon (Rev. 16–19)—a period of time known as the time of *grace*—allows man the opportunity to truly exercise his free will. Before the Cross, mankind was a slave to Satan and had no real ability to express his God-given free will. He was made a captive. (Note: God's workings with mankind in the Old Testament deal primarily with the children of Israel, the nation he formed for himself in order to provide a lineage in which the Messiah, the Christ, would be born. These people were designed to bring the Savior to us, and their laws were created to bring us to the Savior. (See Gal. 3:24.)

Christ's victory at Calvary and his abiding Holy

Spirit now enable us to determine whom we will serve. At the Cross, he offers us the restoration of a fully operative free will. We are no longer forced to serve the enemy. Jesus said, "Now is the time for judgment of this world; now the prince of this world will be driven out" (John 12:31). Later he says that the Holy Spirit will convict the world "in regard to judgment, because the prince of this world now stands condemned" (16:11). In destroying Satan's authority over mankind, Christ made it possible for us to make significant choices. Now, contrary to our lives before Christ came in, we can make the choice not to serve the enemy.

The Cross resulted in Satan's legal defeat, for it was in the shedding of Christ's blood that he triumphed over Satan. "He forgave us all our sins, having canceled the written code, with its regulations, that was against us and that stood opposed to us; he took it away, nailing it to the cross. And having disarmed the powers and authorities, he made a public spectacle of them, triumphing over them by the cross" (Col. 2:13-15).

That triumph was an initial victory. It wasn't the end but rather the beginning of the end. Some of Satan's authority and power is yet to be dealt with. But Paul describes the final victory to the Corinthians. "Then the end will come, when he [Jesus] hands over the kingdom to God the Father after he has destroyed all dominion, authority and power. For he must reign until he has put all his enemies under his feet" (1 Cor. 15:24-25). It is through the Church, the Redeemed, that God chooses to deal with the enemy. The putting down of dominion, authority, and power opposed to God is done, in part, through committed believers to whom he has entrusted his authority (Luke 10:19). We are to continue to fight until the last battle of this age when Christ comes and brings with him the armies of heaven—angels and redeemed men—to fight against

Satan's hordes (Rev. 19:14; 20:4). That battle will usher in the end of this age.

It may seem strange that mankind and Satan share existence in the same realm. It also seems strange that Satan rules over unregenerated mankind and that he has the ability to influence and affect those who serve the Lord. But it is a fact that cannot be denied; it is a reality confirmed by Scripture.

Where Did Satan Get This Power? In Genesis 1:26-30, the Bible tells us that God clearly gave all that he created on earth into man's hands. In essence he said, "Here, I give you this planet. It's yours, rule over it." By the end of chapter 3, however, we find that man had lost his right to rule and was subsequently driven from the garden of Eden, his primary residence. Because of his disobedience to God, the first man, Adam, forfeited the blessings God had given to him. Sin separated man from his Creator and left him powerless against Satan and incapable of ruling earth. Through his disobedience, man literally gave the dominion of the earth to the enemy. With Satan in control, God's blessing was removed and earth became cursed.

As we noted at the beginning of this chapter, when Satan tempted Jesus he claimed that the world was his: "I will give you all their (the kingdoms of the world) authority and splendor, for it has been given to me, and I can give it to anyone I want to. So if you worship me, it will all be yours" (Luke 4:6-7). Satan recalls the time Adam forfeited the deed to earth and further shows that he [Satan] is now so much in control that he can give it to anyone he desires. If this were not true, there would have been no substance to the temptation. But it is true: the enemy rules the earth. And Jesus does not challenge this fact; he simply declines Satan's offer.

In his book, *Prayer Is Invading the Impossible,* Jack Hayford says: "Jesus' denial of Satan's offer is significant not only in his refusal of the lying option afforded him, but also in the fact that he does not challenge Satan's claim to the right of rulership over the kingdoms of this world. The stakes were real and entirely in his control. Jesus was the Outsider."[10]

But Jesus does not remain silent on the subject. He says that the present ruler will be cast out (John 12:31, KJV).

Satan received control of earth through deception; Man lost control through disobedience. That is always the case. Man will always lose something when he disobeys (Gen. 3), then he complains that it wasn't his fault—someone else took his possession away from him. The truth is that through disobedience, man gives away his freedom, his health, his happiness, and his security.

Why Did Satan Rebel? Although the Bible does not give specifics concerning Satan's reasons for his rebellion, we can assume the following: Though we have already mentioned Satan's desire for praise, perhaps at the very core of his waywardness were jealousy and pride. God created Satan, who was at that time known only as Lucifer, and placed him in such a position that he was, no doubt, one of the highest, if not *the* highest, of all the angels. Then when God created man in his own image and likeness, Satan was no longer the center of attention. Not only was there a "new baby" around, but it was a being with God's own generic qualities. The enemy perhaps felt that he was being replaced. And to him, second in line was not acceptable. Milton could be quite accurate when, in his own writings, he quotes Satan as saying, "It is better to rule in hell than to serve in heaven."

Man is perhaps unlike any other of God's creations.

When God created him, he created his own personal family generated by God's very own life. When it became necessary to redeem mankind, the incarnation was possible because of our similarity to the very image and likeness of God (a condition some believe is not found in angels).

God created a people with whom he intended the highest fellowship; a people who were not only created like him, but who were to be totally dependent upon him. So it is possible that Satan's jealousy and pride concerning this new creation became his initial stumbling blocks and soon he was leading the rebellion. Today he continues with an indignation bent on destroying the human race. He has only one plan for you and me: extermination.

Why Has Satan Been Allowed to Continue? There are perhaps many reasons why Satan continues his rampage of earth. Let's look at three possibilities. First, God may be allowing the present struggle to persist to bring Christians "on-the-job training," through prayer, for their eventual rulership with Christ throughout eternity. In this way, we can participate in our own salvation and in the preparation needed for future rulership.

Secondly, in Ecclesiastes 8:11 we read: "When the sentence for a crime is not quickly carried out, the hearts of the people are filled with schemes to do wrong." Our present evil world, unlike any other system we know of, allows the true heart of a person to be established. If God were to bring immediate reward or punishment for every action or deed we committed, we soon would find ourselves acting like Pavlov's dogs. We would respond like robots to electric commands. We would have tremendous conditioned responses, but there would be no heart behind them. The knowledge of instant compensation would never allow a person's true character to be revealed. Some would do good for selfish reasons, while others would do it to avoid penalty. God desires voluntary cooperation. And only patience during tribulation will establish the type of character that will permit a loving relationship with a loving God.

The third possible reason that Satan has been allowed to continue involves learning by experience. There are many things in life that cannot be fully comprehended except by experience. Parents sometimes find themselves in a position where it is best to let older, rebellious children make some mistakes on their own in the hopes that they will see more clearly afterwards. So God, knowing that wayward man will understand his own and the angels' utter failure to produce anything worthwhile outside of a relationship with him, may be letting us stumble through the mistakes we make in this life for our own good.

But regardless of how Satan has received his power as the ruler of the world, it is limited: "For there is no power but of God: and the powers that be are ordained of God" (Rom. 13:1). Though for a time the enemy has power here on earth, his authority is not outside of that which God has ordained. God still is, and always will be, sovereign.

Therefore, until Satan is finally put down we are engaged, whether we like it or not, in spiritual warfare. However, there are many who have not yet joined God's "army"; they are still captives of Satan and are not free to "fight the good fight of the faith" (1 Tim. 6:12). We shall soon discover the identity of these captives and how they might be set free.

NOTES

1. C. Leslie Miller, *All About Angels* (Ventura, Calif.: Regal Books, 1973), 81-82.

2. There are other explanations as to the origin of demons. I have chosen the most common and easiest to understand since the Bible is not totally clear on this point. One interesting account is found in the book of Enoch where they are said to be the departed spirits of the giants of the Old Testament. These giants, from this same account, were the product of sexual relationships between men and angels.
3. I believe that both Isaiah 14 and Ezekiel 28 do in fact refer directly to the enemy of our soul. What seems only to be a challenge to individual cities is really a dispute with the unseen power that controls these cities. What seems to be directed only toward earthly kings is obviously, upon closer examination, much more than that. Isaiah talks of far greater goals and motives than an earthly king or his city have ever had (vv. 13-14). Ezekiel describes a person whose character widely exceeds that of the king of Tyre. Was the king of Tyre "full of wisdom and perfect in beauty" (Ezek. 28:12, KJV)? Was he in the Garden of Eden (v. 13)? Was he an anointed angel (v. 14)? Was he ever on the "holy mountain of God" or did he "walk back and forth in the midst of fiery stones" or was he perfect in all his ways (vv. 14-15)? No. Not one of these descriptions would ever fit any natural king. But they do fit Satan, both scripturally and historically. Our traditional understanding of the enemy has changed little in hundreds of years. This, along with a rise in the occult where biblical terminology is further affirmed, gives credence to the presence of Satan in these two chapters of Scripture.
4. Lewis Sperry Chafer, *Satan* (New York: Gospel Publishing House, 1909), Introduction.
5. Because of the English translation of Isaiah 45:7, where it refers to God as creating evil, some people may misunderstand both God's intention in this verse and an aspect of his nature. The Hebrew word used in that verse for create is *bara*, which means "to create, dispatch, do, or make." The Hebrew word for evil is *ra*, which is translated as "adversity, calamity, and affliction"—not as "sin." God has never sinned nor has he created sin, but he does allow adversity, calamity, and affliction to come as a result of the law of sowing and reaping. His intention, then, in Isaiah 45:7, is to warn men that they will experience suffering and sorrow if they insist on sinning.
6. Ibid., 17.
7. Ethel Barrett, *The Great Conflict* (Ventura, Calif.: Regal Books, 1969), Prologue.
8. Chafer, *Satan*, 22.
9. C. S. Lewis, *The Screwtape Letters* (New York: Macmillan, 1961), vii.
10. Jack W. Hayford, *Prayer Is Invading the Impossible*, (Plainfield, N.J.: Logos International, 1977), 22.

TWO

Realizing We Have Been Captured

Within mankind, there is kind of an intuitive knowledge that points to the existence of God and that furthermore realizes we are somehow incorrectly separated from him. In art, literature, and religion we often see the expression of this knowledge.

"Dr. Trumball, in that masterful study of ancient sacrifices, *Blood-Covenant*, points out that all the peoples of antiquity, of whatever race or country, practiced sacrifices in one form or another, either of animals or of human beings. He wisely gathers from a study that took him to the sacrificial altars of countless aborigines that an instinct so universal and so deep-seated reveals that man—in his blind gropings after God and moved by the deepest intuitions of the race—has attempted to establish harmonious relations with the Divine only on the basis of death."[1]

From here, however, mankind becomes confused over the real problem of life and what to do about it. This confusion existed universally until God was revealed to us in the person of Jesus Christ. There is no longer any mystery about what is wrong with humanity: we are lost and bound by sin because of our rebellion. Now we must learn from God the processes and procedures necessary to free us from bondage and to bring us back to our intended relationship with our Creator. He wants us to know what went wrong in the beginning and what he is willing to do to help correct the situation, and then what we must do to participate in our own deliverance.

When Adam and Eve disobeyed God in the Garden, it constituted rebellion against him. But rebellion goes much deeper than the initial sin[2] of doing something not approved by God. For when Adam and Eve disobeyed they did not just strain a relationship; their defiance pushed God out of their lives, thus opening themselves and all their descendants to the influence and subsequent control of an entire realm of other created beings. These beings were angels who, with the free will God had given them, had at some point in eternity past decided not to stay in subjection to their Creator. All mankind, therefore, through Adam and Eve, joined demonic rebellion and became Satan's slaves.

But sadly, few of us recognize our bondage. We often are not aware of our slavery to Satan until we recognize real freedom. Simon Peter is certainly a classical case. He considered himself to be of some stature because Christ had called him. Only after Jesus said to him, "Out of my sight, Satan," and "This very night, before the rooster crows, you will disown me three times," was Peter eventually able to see his bondage. Then, when he was truly converted, he became a powerful man of God.

Likewise, every person born to a slave is a slave. Since Adam became a slave (through disobedience), every one of his descendants has been born a slave. So Satan continues to be in control of all of lost humanity. Every child born is his subject. And we continue, by choice, to reinforce this slavery condition—even though there is now a way out.

As stated earlier, not only did the first man and woman fall into bondage because they listened to Satan's lie, they also forfeited everything God had given them. Through disobedience they handed their authority over to Satan, forfeiting their right to "rule over" this domain and establishing Satan as the ruler of this world.

The Apostle John in his first Epistle tells his readers that now "the whole world is under the control of the evil one" (1 John 5:10). Man walked away from his Creator and united with rebel demons in a resistance force against him. Once man disobeyed, he was further enticed to become defiant; he coupled his disobedience with outright rebellion. His rebellion then caused more disobedience, which in turn caused more rebellion. And that vicious cycle still continues.

Generally when we think of sin, we think of not doing what is right (sins of omission) or doing what is wrong (sins of commission). It seldom dawns on us that defiance, which is a more serious aspect of disobedience, is the major hindrance to establishing and maintaining a relationship with God. Sinning is not the key issue. Although sin is a problem we must confront, God has a solution for wrong actions. The real issue is rebellion. In spite of these facts we, as a lost race, still choose to defy God. We choose to rebel, saying, "Leave me alone. Let me do it my way. I can make it on my own." The Fall of man has instilled within us a nature contrary to God's original design, one that has developed because of Satan's influence and subtle deceptions.

Adam and Eve did not become as completely bad when they first sinned as we see the world today. Quite the contrary. It took Satan a while to corrupt them with what would eventually become a totally defiled nature. Step by step, mankind learned escalating degrees of rebellion as he continued to choose evil over good, disobedience over obedience.

Then, once jealousy entered the human race, it produced murder. Once murder entered, it produced vengeance. And jealousy, murder, and vengeance in one person soon spread to others. As quickly as Satan could get man to respond he infected him with evil until he had extended perversity to every facet of human existence. Now the sin nature is so much a part of us that righteousness is foreign. (God confirms this when he says that there is not a single person who is righteous, not one—and that all our so-called righteousnesses are as filthy rags, good for nothing.) Now we oppose God in every way, strutting before him and asking, "How can God know?" (Ps. 73:11). We think that "the Lord has forsaken the land, the Lord does not see" (Ezek. 9:9). We have become proud, arrogant, and boastful. We exist in a state of rebellion. By our fallen nature we continue to choose to sin; we would rather be one of those with "a turned back" (like the rich young ruler) than one with "a bowed head" (like the woman who washed Jesus' feet with her tears).

In order to more fully understand the salvation that is available through Jesus Christ, we need to understand the extent of our broken relationship with God. There are two aspects to our defiance and opposition towards him. The first is our outright disobedience to his commands. Let's call this *sinning in the flesh*.[3] It involves the direction of our actions.

The second aspect deals with our rebellious attitudes. Let's call this aspect, which is largely the result of joining the opposition, *spiritual sin*. It is this spiritual sin that develops our old nature. *The old (Adamic) nature* refers to the nature man acquired when he fell away from God. The original fall gives it the name *Adamic* after

Adam. This is the nature (which has much to do with the spirit) that comes from being programmed by the enemy's lies and deceptions. As animals acquire certain characteristics over time (evidenced by the many different breeds of dogs and their individual behaviors), man since Adam's time has been carefully indoctrinated by demon spirits. Thus he has acquired certain characteristics. The old nature refers to the nature in man to use the deeds of the body for sinful purposes and to cooperate with the enemy.

SINS OF THE FLESH

Much of the action-oriented sin we are involved in is a consequence of the "out of control" appetites of our bodies. Our inborn separation from God creates within us a nature that adversely affects our natural senses. The drives associated with survival—thirst, hunger, rest, sex—were all given to us by God. It was his plan that man would fulfill these drives in a wholesome and pleasurable way and, in so doing, enjoy his earthly existence while keeping his spiritual existence intact. When man sinned, his spiritual life with God was cut off and he was left with "body drives" that became predominant. Much of his life was then given over to fulfilling these drives with little concern for the needs of his spirit. This response to our body drives is universal. If the body says, "I'm hungry," we drop everything to meet that need. If it says, "I'm cold," we turn up the thermostat. The minute it speaks we respond, quite frequently without giving a thought to whether or not our actions are right.

If our spirit—a part of our makeup that we will discuss later—were dominant and in tune with God, we would not want to do wrong. Without that dominance—because we are separated from God when we are outside of Christ—our powerful sin nature amplifies the desires of the body, turns them toward evil, and forces us into error. Often our spirit tells us what is right and, inwardly, we want to do good, but something drives us into wrongdoing. And that something is the sin nature that lives within us and produces evil actions—or *sins* in the plural. So our wrong deeds are the result of inner wrong, and something needs to happen to correct this situation from within. In order to make the fruit good, it is necessary to heal the root. The very nature of sin must be dealt with before sins can be conquered. This will be more fully explained in chapter 5.

Note the significant difference between sin and sins. *Sin,* singular, describes our inner nature, passed on to us from Adam because of the Fall and brought to light and made powerful because of the Old Testament Law (see Rom. 7:8-9). *Sins,* plural, refers to the specific wrong actions and deeds. It is sin (singular) which causes sins or sinning (plural). Generally speaking, *sin* is attitude and *sins* are action.

Of course, unregenerated man laughs at the thought of sin; he pictures it as a concept presented by a cold, distant Creator and preached from pulpits with the intent of eliminating all the fun in life. An article from the Associated Press illustrates my point. It quotes a young man who believes God to be some sort of tyrant with a penchant against pleasure: "I often think of Satan as a cool dude. Since he controls one part of the supernatural, he tends to let you be on your own, to do what you want, whereas God has his own rules on how you're supposed to live. They're kind of binding. He wants to put you in a jail cell, to control you."[4]

It's true, sin does let you do your own thing—and it certainly is appealing. It provides momentary pleasure. But the lasting effects not only hinder life on earth but also have eternal consequences. When we sin we are trying to do something we were not created to do. Sin won't work. It's going against God's very plan for our existence. Just as God didn't plan for fish to live above water or man to live below it, so the things he warns against in his Word are those that can't possibly work. God calls these unworkable things sin. And it is his Word that determines what is unworkable, what is sin.

In times of great thirst when pure water is not available, some people have resorted to drinking sea water—with deadly consequences. While it is water, it cannot be drunk safely because of the heavy salt content; it won't work for quenching thirst. Indeed, it is deadly. So it is with sin.

However, if the lost man is bound by sin, and sin forces him to do wrong, then isn't it true that he does not have a choice? And if he has no choice but to do things that are bad, why does the unsaved man sometimes have the inner strength to quit smoking or drinking or any number of other things that he determines to do? To answer this we must realize that even in our lost condition we still have some inner strength, and we can direct that toward a particular problem with some positive results. Often, however, our strength is not sufficient to complete the task, and we find ourselves once again doing the things we want to avoid. Also, our strength is far from sufficient to confront *all* the problems we face. If our own power of choice were as strong as we would like to believe, then we could choose righteousness in every case, walk away from sin, and be totally free. And we would not need help . . . or a Savior.

Paul the apostle certifies in Romans 7 that it is the "law of sin" that has brought us into bondage. If there is a law that forces us to do wrong, then how can we operate freely? How can we truly express our own will? The answer is simply that we can't because we, as a result of our separation from God, have been taken captive by the devil. Paul desires that "they will come to their senses and escape from the trap of the devil, who has taken them captive to do his will" (2 Tim. 2:26).

So what is the law of sin? Basically it is being forced to miss the mark. It would be like someone bumping an archer every time he released the arrow. When Adam first sinned and God's presence left him, he became incapable of doing right. With Satan's constant influence, everything Adam did was, in some way, not done right. He was programmed for error; he became conditioned to do wrong.

Let us stop here for a moment. A proper balance is needed here so that we won't try to justify our sin by blaming Satan for our condition. The first man's choice brought about our captivity; our own stubborness continues to hold us in bondage. So we are sinners from conception (Ps. 51:5) and sinners by behavior. In that sense, then, we cannot blame Satan for all sin. We, as a race, must take responsibility for our own actions despite the enemy's hand in encouraging the inception of the law of sin and his continued influence in individual deeds of wrongdoing. As Harold Lindsell explains: "Adam's transgression brought physical and spiritual death, as well as sin, to him and his posterity. The devil was the agent in Adam's fall, but Adam himself, and he alone, was responsible. His choice could not be, and was not, forced on him either by God or by Satan. As a result of the sins of Satan and Adam, the earth and the whole cosmos have been affected. Satan, the fallen angels, and man have joined forces against their Creator and are linked together in the struggle."[5]

Our problems are caused by an evil heart that has sinned against God. We are not, as some sociologists would have us believe, the product of our environment and therefore blameless. We cannot blame society, Satan, or God for our difficulties. We must bear the responsibility personally. And only when we are willing to own up to our sin will God step in to help us.

Then do we, as fallen humanity, truly have free will? Yes, we do. We have free will to choose. But what we don't always have is the power to carry out the choices we make. The capacity for choice is within us and, in many cases, we can choose between right and wrong. However, the original choice to disobey now keeps us from carrying out subsequent choices we desire to make. We may do well for a while but eventually we experience failure. Both sin and Satan will violate our free will as often as possible. When Jesus said that Satan is the "prince" of this world (John 12:31), he affirmed that those outside of Christ are slaves to him. Only Christ can free us. And ultimately that is the one and only free choice we have—to accept or reject Jesus Christ.

SINS OF THE SPIRIT

Beyond the sin of disobeying God's commands is the more formal sin of rebellion, prodded by our nature of sin. At this deeper point, not only do we enter into the sins of the flesh (see note 2 at the end of this chapter), but we enter into the sins of the spirit.[6] Whether we are aware of it or not, we become allied with demon spirits since there are only two sides in this spiritual warfare (there is no neutrality).

This does not mean that every non-Christian is wrapped up with all kinds of demons, although many are. It does not mean that demons are lurking behind every bush or hiding down every corridor waiting to pounce on people. It does mean, however, that demon forces control the world organization and that anyone who is not a part of the kingdom of

God through Jesus Christ is subject to Satan's system. Jesus said either a person is for him or he is against him (Matt. 12:30). There is no middle ground.

We want to consider two areas, then, in which sin operates: first, the area of doing things we were not created to do—sins of the flesh; and, second, the area of joining the opposition, the rebellion—spiritual sin. God never treats either area lightly. However, grace often is applied to the first area, the sins of the flesh. God is a gracious God and forgives when we first repent (Acts 17:30). After we become his children, he continues to forgive us when we confess our sins (1 John 1:9). In fact, God wants us to come to him for forgiveness so that we can be free from the guilt that comes from unconfessed or unacknowledged sin.

Rebellion, on the other hand, is a different matter. It is showing an attitude of defiance as we yield ourselves to the ongoing influence of the demonic realm. We often do this by simply neglecting God, acting as if he did not exist. Whereas it might be argued that we commit sins of the flesh because the flesh is weak, rebellion is something we freely choose to do ourselves, making us all that much more Satan's slaves—and giving us a nature bent on pleasing the flesh in sinful ways.

To illustrate the difference between the sins of the flesh and the sin of rebellion, consider two boys whose mothers told them to stay out of mud puddles on their way to school after a spring rain. The first boy respects his mother's wishes and wants to please her, but the puddles would be fun to splash in and there's just enough mud in them to make it exciting. In a weak moment he jumps in and ends up covered with mud. The second boy, however, has no intention of obeying his mother. He says, "I don't care what anyone says. I'm going to hit those puddles and no one is going to stop me." Both boys were guilty of a transgression. The first boy yielded to temptation and sinned; the second boy, however, exhibited a rebellion that represents a much more severe problem. Such direct defiance is hard on any parent. Likewise, deliberate defiance is difficult for God to deal with because he will not force his will upon us. He respects our right to choose.

Rebellion is a major problem that each person must resolve. If it is not dealt with properly in this life through Jesus Christ, it will tragically continue for eternity. Some believe that suicide will cure its pain. Not so. Some believe that death ends its horrible effects. It doesn't. The damage to one's spirit because of rebellion will carry on past the door of death (Luke 16:19-31).

Since rebellion is primarily a spiritual problem, it must be faced on a spiritual level. Only one Spirit can conquer the Evil One who incited the rebellion and that is the Holy Spirit of God. How can our spirits contact his Spirit? Through a mediator: "For there is one God and one mediator between God and men, the man Christ Jesus, who gave himself as a ransom for all men" (1 Tim. 2:5-6).

The Mediator. Without truly understanding who Jesus Christ is, why he came, what he accomplished, and the extent of the problems we face, it becomes virtually impossible to fight the spiritual war at hand with any degree of effectiveness.

As previously mentioned, God originally gave the dominion of earth to mankind. But when we sinned, we transferred our legal control of this planet to Satan and found ourselves living in a realm dominated by the enemy. We became Satan's slaves, deeply subjected to his influence. We were bound in every way and incapable of freeing ourselves. Thus, in

47

God's beautiful plan, he became the man that would free all others. This he could do quite easily, perhaps, because of our similarity to his image and likeness.

In his plan he would have to be introduced into the human race in a way in which he would not inherit Adam's original sin. Since sin is passed on by conception (see Ps. 51:5) and since it causes slavery, every person born of normal parents would be bound by sin and also be a slave to the enemy. Jesus would have to come in a way in which sin would not be passed to his nature, and this could only be accomplished by the virgin birth. Without such a birth by supernatural conception, he would have inherited Adam's sin and been disqualified from entering the battle against the enemy.

But Jesus *was* qualified to enter the battle because, although he was God, he was also a man. And although he was a man, he was sinless. Because Jesus was born of a virgin through the Holy Spirit, he was the first man since Adam to be born free of sin's grasp. Because he was free of that grasp, he was not Satan's slave.

From the moment Jesus was born until his death on the Cross, Satan did everything he could to destroy him. The enemy's basic desire was to get Jesus to disobey the Father. Then this second Adam would also be brought into bondage. But Jesus was aware of the ploy and set his heart toward total obedience to God the Father. "Whatever I see the Father do, I do" (John 5:19). He was saying, "I am going to be totally obedient. I will not sin." And he was obedient, right on through the times of suffering, all the way to the Cross—and death (Phil. 2:8; Heb. 5:7-9).

Here now was a man over whom Satan had no legal control or authority. As Adam had power to resist Satan before he (Adam) sinned, so now there was a second Adam with power against the enemy. We must understand that Christ's power came through his sinless nature and not his deity. Deity does, however, play a major role in overcoming because it is man empowered by God (indwelt by the Holy Spirit)—along with angels inspired by God (we do not know if they can be filled with the Holy Spirit as can a man)—through whom the battle is being won. Sinful man could not be empowered because he was separated. Christ could be empowered, anointed, and filled with the Holy Spirit to overcome Satan because he had no sin—either by birth or through his own flesh—to separate him from God the Father.

When we accept the sacrifice of Calvary, we are united with God and he is then willing to justify us and empower us to fight sin and Satan. We did not receive our justification by any goodness of our own but by simply accepting the goodness of Christ. Being justified, however, does not mean we no longer sin. Rather, it means that in Christ we no longer *practice* sin. Sin, even in the life of a Christian, still has a separating effect and reduces our inner power against Satan and his forces. The good news is that "if we confess our sins, he is faithful and just and will forgive us our sins and purify us from all unrighteousness" (1 John 1:9).

Christ lived an overcoming life with the help of the Holy Spirit, and we are able to do the same. We can be empowered, just as he was. Remember, he promised to give us power similar to and even greater than the power he had when he was here on earth (John 14:12). In John 14:16 we are told how that will come about. He said that when he went away he would send the Comforter, the Holy Spirit, to come into us and abide with us forever. So it is the Holy Spirit that gives us the power to overcome.

Of Men and Angels. Jesus became the means by which God was able to save mankind from Satan's bondage. God's plan was to use a man to deliver mankind and, since no one else was qualified, he became that individual himself. By becoming a man, he could legally fight against rebellion. I say legally because God made the rules; he would not arbitrarily go against man's own will to rebel. He would not simply step in and clean up the mess as if nothing had happened. In his capacity as God, it appears he had limited himself in dealing with the free will he had created. But as a human being, without the power of his deity, there were no restrictions. He could fight—and fight he did.

God is not like some parents who run around cleaning up after their children and, in so doing, fail to teach them responsibility. God could have wiped sin and rebellion out instantly, but in order to preserve free will, he didn't. Make no mistake, sin and rebellion will be put down. But that may come more from unrebellious created beings than from God himself. It is the love for allegiance to righteousness and a hatred of that which is an affront to God that cries out for redress of this present evil world. Redeemed man and unfallen angels are demanding righteousness and a halt to injustice and inequity. We cannot abide what Satan, his demon angels, and unregenerated man have perpetrated. This is why we can "fight a good fight" and why prayer changes things.

The judgment of Satan and the disposition of rebellion is, of course, in God's hands. But is it possible that it could not also be largely in the hands of unrebellious, unfallen angels and regenerated men? If God creates something and it rebels and then God steps in and "wipes it out," are we not merely robots and puppets? Cannot God then be labeled arbitrary and capricious? Could it not be that the myriad of

free-will beings who chose not to rebel have peti-
tioned God for the putting down of this insurrection?
Could it not be that they have said to God, "You tell
us what to do and where to begin and we will do it.
We will do it because it is *our* desire that rebellion
ceases to exist."

In the Old Testament where there are accounts of
many wars, you will find that it is necessary for men
and angels to join God in fighting evil. Before God
would judge Egypt, his people had to ask for help
and Moses had to be obedient to him to bring about
deliverance. Joseph, David, Esther, Daniel, and many
others can be listed as those God used to win victories. But they had to "will" righteousness first. Specifically, angels such as Michael and Gabriel also
play a part.

As St. Augustine said, "Without God, man cannot.
Without man, God will not." Angels and mankind
who are in league with God want to submit and be
obedient to God as much as those who have sinned
want to rebel. Perhaps a great deal of what God does
is based upon *their* desire for a peaceful universe
where God rules and reigns. They want God's will to
be foremost, so he makes it known and they carry it
out.

Somehow, we have the idea that the battle over
earth is between God and Satan. It isn't! The battle is
between those who have submitted to God and those
who have rebelled against him. It's true, we are not
fighting other people. However, those of our own
households as well as friends and acquaintances
may turn against us when we turn to Christ. So
while, for the most part, the battle rages in the heavenlies, it is nevertheless a battle between submission
and rebellion.

Neither is the warfare just between good and evil.
In the realm of right and wrong the battle exists

between walking in the spirit and walking in the flesh. Good or evil become a consequence of that walk.

In describing the holy angels in their pursuit of righteousness, it must not be implied that they are mindless, spineless individuals operating with computer-like movements—although swift and gracious—and programmed by God according to his will and without their consent. The idea that angels are without a will, mind, and emotions does not take into account that many have rebelled (2 Pet. 2:4; Jude 6; Rev. 12:4), that they experience joy when one is born into God's kingdom (Luke 15:10), and that numbers of them fight furiously in the realm of darkness. As we consider angels, then, we are not pondering some sort of automaton. We are looking at created beings with personalities and thoughts of their own. And those angels who are submitted to God follow him because that is their choice.

Whichever way we look at the struggle, it becomes apparent that God's angels and redeemed men have authority and power to fight. They affect the battle. This does not detract one ounce from God's sovereignty; rather it emphasizes God's desire not to violate the free will he so carefully gave us in order to make us individuals.

So we are commissioned to fight, not in our own strength but in the power and might of a living Savior. We are to be an extension of his ministry against the enemy.

It may be that some ungodly people will be surprised on the judgment day when they have to reckon with the testimony of men and angels who were personally affected by their rebellion. Unless a person receives Jesus as his or her own personal Savior, making Jesus that person's advocate (lawyer) (1 John 2:1), he or she may face a court battle in which the testimony of Christians and angels become that person's undoing. Right now, multitudes of redeemed men and women would be willing to testify to the damage they have personally suffered because of divorce, rape, murder, and other forms of evil in a society where godlessness in judicial decisions, television programming, legislative action, and police enforcement has contributed to a rise in satanic activity. It may be that many people will be shocked not only that they are going to trial but also at who testifies against them.

When man rebelled he had no way of getting back under the protection of God by himself. God would have to do something. Therefore he separated himself from the power of his deity in order to come in the form of a man to rescue lost humanity. Once here, he operated against Satan with his sinlessness as his defense and his death as his weapon: "Being in the very nature God, Jesus did not consider equality with God something to be grasped, but made himself nothing, taking the very nature of a servant, being made in human likeness. And being found in appearance as a man, he humbled himself and became obedient to death—even death on a cross!" (Phil. 2:6-8).

Once Jesus fought and won the battle for man's salvation, once he began the process for repossessing earth's dominion, mankind was no longer obligated to be Satan's slave. Jesus, as a sinless human being and not in his capacity as God, had fulfilled all legal demands for justice and righteousness. The sacrifice of his blood met God's conditions for mankind's release from both sin and Satan. All that the enemy possessed in rulership over man has once again become the possession of Jesus Christ. Sinless humanity once again took control of earth.

But, as has always been the case, God will never force men or angels into anything. Although Satan no longer has a legal right over us, we still have to *choose* to submit to God. We still have to be wooed back by God's love. And so Jesus now makes the offer, "Here I am! I stand at the door and knock. If anyone hears . . ." (Rev. 3:20). Jesus came to bring new life and to begin the removal of satanic rebellion. But much of the battle was yet to come, and it was to be the responsibility of Jesus' followers as he directed them from his position of power next to the Father.

When Jesus looks for "applicants," he must deal first with the will of lost humanity. He extends his arms to anyone who will give up allegiance to Satan and self-willed waywardness. For the multitudes who come to him, he becomes their Captain in the fight against the world, the flesh, and the devil. For those who don't come, he still holds out his nail-scarred hands of love. Someone has said, "Love never reaches out to give but that it does so with wounded hand."

Redeemed man has a tremendous responsibility to tell those who have not heard. The Holy Spirit is then responsible to convict and convince those who hear the message that they are lost in their sin and need to accept God's way of salvation. By cooperation, we become "God's fellow workers" (1 Cor. 3:9) in turning man from his rebellion.

"WHAT MUST I DO?"

What it cost God to "buy back" his creations is more than most of us are capable of fully comprehending. It would be easier if we could, for even a moment, understand that God has *suffered* to save us.

But how do we follow through? How do we contact the Almighty God?

After God wrought a mighty miracle on behalf of

Paul and Silas while they were incarcerated in Philippi, the amazed Philippian jailer asked a most important question, "Men," he said, "what must I do to be saved?" (Acts 16:30).

Came the reply, "Believe on the Lord Jesus, and you will be saved—you and your household" (Acts 16:31). This word *believe* was never intended to convey a simple mental acceptance of Jesus Christ; it was meant to open the door to a genuine heartfelt transaction of repentance and faith. By turning away from sin, we confess to the world that Jesus Christ is now our Lord and Master. To believe means that we acknowledge Christ is the way for us to be delivered from Satan's bondage and that he is the only way we can transfer allegiance from Satan to God. And this is possible only because of the blood of Jesus Christ. At this point we allow him to enter our lives.

Sin can be forgiven only on the basis of shed blood. This is why animal sacrifice was necessary in the Old Testament as a way of covering sin. Christ's blood shed once and for all is now sufficient to satisfy God's wrath toward all unrighteousness. Christ's blood, however, will be of no avail in destroying the enmity between an individual and God until that individual applies the sacrifice to himself by asking Christ to enter into his life. When Christ enters we take on a "new nature," God's nature. Christ's Spirit literally comes to dwell in our human spirit (Col. 1:27). When we accept Christ we remove ourselves from the kingdom of darkness and all of its bondage to the kingdom of light and all of its liberty (Acts 26:18; Gal. 1:4).

"Only believe," or "If you accept Jesus as your personal Savior" may be phrases some find hard to grasp. It is possible for a person to go through the mechanics of salvation during a crisis situation and not truly be saved. If they eventually do experience being "born again" (John 3:3) through the revelation of the Holy Spirit, they understand that salvation is a spiritual experience that is sealed in the heart. When we approach it only on an intellectual level, it falls far short of the life-changing encounter it is designed to be.

Even though some people do not grasp the idea of salvation, we who are redeemed still have the responsibility of telling the world about a *personal Savior*, a Savior who literally enters lives on an individual basis. Yet the world (especially the cults and the occult) continues to attack the idea of a Savior being personal. By taking out the word *personal*, the world does not have to be concerned about coming to a decision concerning Jesus. The word *personal* acknowledges free will and demands a decision to either accept or reject Christ as God's only way to salvation.

To call Jesus a "savior" without the personal element makes him only one in a long line of saviors. If Christ is only one of many saviors, then, to be effective, all of them had to be born sinless as he was. This is the only way they could be free from Satan's grasp. But if all the others were sinless, where is that record? All of them were born of human parents. All were conceived in sin and born in iniquity (Ps. 51:5); therefore they all were sinful and not qualified to do battle against Satan for the deliverance of mankind. But herein is the beautiful plan of God: mankind was rescued by a sinless man who was also God.

Jesus was born sinless into Satan's realm. He was an outsider. That Christ came from a distant place to invade earth, bringing light and life into a realm filled with death and darkness, is somewhat difficult to grasp. But it happened. Christ's mission was to establish his kingdom here on earth and, in the process, restore to us the control we had lost. Prophecy had already established that he would come, and many watched for him. But no one had expected that he would come to establish his kingdom first in the human heart. When he moved to this planet his plan was to move "inside" those who were waiting to receive him. Jack Hayford adds:

> A planet acclimated to death and dying, to sickness and suffering, to weakness and failure, to sin and strife, to war and heartbreak, to trouble and tragedy, to division and divorce—to accepting the insolubility of the impossible—was being invaded.
>
> The invading force was only one. But that One was the Creator of all, who from the beginning had calculated a plan which would not only mystify the enemy and release his prisoners; it would introduce the redeemed to a pathway of sharing with Him in His conquest.
>
> So it began to happen.
>
> Life was beginning to infect the poisoned planet with health. Love was beginning to flow purely into the muddied cisterns of man's being.
>
> But when a planet's inhabitants are accustomed to fear and death and when the liar who rules them has adequately convinced them that these traits and all that goes with them are normal, such an invasion will only stimulate violent resistance which only violence overcomes.[7]

Jesus Christ was more than a radical. Yes, he was an invader. He came as an expeditionary force of one to conquer planet earth. And since that time the resistance has been reacting. A war has developed and violence has broken out. "And from the days of John the Baptist until now, the kingdom of heaven has been forcefully advancing, and forceful men lay hold of it" (Matt. 11:12). How do we prepare ourselves for this forceful advance? In the next chapter we'll look at ways to prepare for battle.

NOTES

1. F. J. Huegel, *Bone of His Bone* (Grand Rapids: Zondervan, 1940), 44.
2. Sin, biblically speaking, is "missing the mark," such as an archer who shoots at a target and misses. It is therefore an action and not a concept or an idea. When we talk about the nature of sin in humanity, we are talking about people who have been programmed to always miss the mark. This happens because we do not have the relationship with our Creator that is necessary for being on target. When we look at sin as a nebulous, ethereal element that Satan has brought to mankind, we fail to see it for what it really is: missing God's intended purpose.

   When Satan sinned he missed the mark. He went outside of the parameters God set for maintaining an orderly universe. Satan went outside of God's plans for his existence.

   It is certainly true that Satan tricked man into committing sin, but he didn't create sin in mankind. Satan created his own sin and man did likewise. Satan may have been first but that is really immaterial. It was through Adam that sin entered the human race and not through the enemy. In this light, the human race becomes responsible for its own sin. Satan influenced it but man created it by himself through his own disobedience.
3. For the purposes of this study, the word *flesh* refers to the cooperation of the senses of the body with the soul when they produce actions displeasing to God and missing his plan and purpose for us.
4. Oxnard, *Press Courier*, April 1984.
5. Harold Lindsell, *The World, the Flesh, and the Devil* (Minneapolis, Minn.: World Wide Publications, 1973), 13.
6. *Sins of the Spirit.* When man fell, he not only broke fellowship with God, but he began to cooperate with the enemy of his soul. All such cooperation is spiritual sin and forms an evil nature in us.
7. Hayford, *Prayer Is Invading the Impossible*, 22.

THREE

Preparing for Battle

Dr. Martyn Lloyd-Jones once said that Christianity "is far too often presented as a remedy for all our problems—'Come to the clinic and we'll give you all the loving care and attention that you need to help you with your problems.'" But, he continues, "In the Bible I find a barracks, not a hospital. It is not a doctor you need but a drill sergeant. Here we are on the parade ground slouching around. A doctor won't help us. It is discipline we need. We need to listen to our Sergeant. 'Yield not to temptation but yield yourselves to God.' This is the trouble with the Church today; there is too much of the hospital element; they have lost sight of the great battle."[1]

I recognize this view represents only one side of the coin. Charles Swindoll in his book *Dropping Your Guard* shares the other.

> What if your wife is an alcoholic? Or your son recently told you he's a practicing homosexual?
> Let's say your husband just walked out . . . or what if he is sexually abusing your two daughters? Or you?
> Who can you turn to if you just got fired? . . . Or you

just got out of jail? . . . Or your 15-year-old daughter told you last night that she was pregnant? . . . Or you beat your kids and you're scared—and ashamed? . . . Or you can't cope with your drug habit any longer? . . . Or you need professional help because you're near a breakdown?

Do you know what you need? You need a shelter. A place of refuge. A few folks who can help you, listen to you, introduce you, once again, to ". . . the Father of mercies, the God of all comfort; who comforts us in all our affliction" (2 Cor. 1:3-4). Christianity may be "like a mighty army," but we often handle our troops in a weird way. We're the only outfit I've ever heard of who shoots their wounded.[2]

Since we can see that even in war there must be places to run to, places of refuge, what should be the position of the Church? Hospital or boot camp? The answer is both. Some people need to be doctored until they are strong enough to fight. But a very serious question still remains. Do most churches move people through the healing process to prepare them for battle? Does a vision of "all-out warfare" exist? I wonder. Such a vision would encompass more than just preaching. It would contain a training plan to help soldiers enter the battle properly.

In this chapter, then, we will discuss the part of the training program that involves the soldier himself.

KNOWING WHERE THE BATTLE BEGINS

Before we can discover how to prepare to fight in this spiritual warfare we must talk about our own makeup—how God has made us. When we know how we are put together, then we are better able to utilize the part of us that must fight the battles.

A common understanding of the makeup of man considers him to be constructed in two parts—body and soul. The body is thought to be the outer, tangible part, while the soul is the inner, intangible part. This observation, however, appears to lack something scripturally. It fails to acknowledge another inner, intangible aspect of humanity—the *spirit*. If we ignore the existence of the spirit-part or if we assume it to be the same as the soul, we may remain confused about our spiritual lives and therefore about spiritual warfare.

The Word of God teaches that we are tri-part creations, including body, soul, and spirit.[3]

It is important that we see these parts as determining function *more* than seeing them as substance. Our goal in this chapter is to define these aspects of our existence. Paul introduces us to this theme in 1 Thessalonians 5:23 where he says: "May your whole spirit, soul, and body be kept blameless at the coming of our Lord Jesus Christ." Here is one of life's primary purposes—that we are to be kept blameless until we see Jesus. But we must see that Paul indicates we must consider three specific areas to accomplish this—spirit, soul, and body. And this is a theme we readily discover in other passages also.

Genesis 2:7 describes this trichotomy of man. We read, "And the Lord God formed man from the dust of the ground [body] and breathed into his nostrils the breath of life [spirit] and man *became* a living being [soul]." Here we discover that God formed Adam's body from ground elements and "breathed into his nostrils"; Adam's soul thus was a product of the uniting of body and spirit.

It appears Adam's soul was formed so that he could function in both the material and the spirit realms. The soul allowed his human spirit to operate in his physical body. The body, therefore, became the temple for this new spiritual being. Here now was spirit entering dust. But spirit and dust together were not sufficient for man's active expression and operation. It was like setting an engine in a car body without the necessary gears to transfer the power to the wheels. The addition of the soul added a transmission and made it possible for the two totally dissimilar parts, body and spirit, to function in harmony.

We operate, for the most part, out of *body* awareness. That is, much of what we do, the decisions we make, the things we think about, and the feelings generated from within all revolve around our body senses. We are conscious of pain, hunger, heat or cold, pleasure, our appearance, and other needs and desires of our bodies. As we talk of the body we are referring basically to its needs, wants, desires, and senses and not just inanimate particles put together to form hands or feet.

Our *souls* embrace our wills, minds, and emotions. These three elements are necessary for a spiritual being to dwell in a physical body. They are necessary for operating in a material world and are furthermore the essence of our personalities.

And our *spirits* have to do with perception (higher spiritual awareness), conviction (being convinced of truth by the Holy Spirit), and fellowship (communion with God in prayer).

The Body—Senses. The psalmist says that we are fearfully and wonderfully made (Ps. 139:14). When God took man from the dust He literally used the elements found in the soil to compose his body. Our bodies consist of salt, iodine, calcium, carbon, iron, and many other elements.

Consider the amazing makeup of our bodies. For example, the body has 206 bones; more than 650 muscles; nearly 12 billion nerve cells; 20,000 hairs in the inner ear to tune in sound; a heart that beats about 70 times a minute pumping about 5 ounces of blood per stroke for a total of 4,000 gallons a day; 2 million sweat glands; lungs containing 400 million air sacs which pump 12,000 quarts of air daily; and an electronic system that keeps the five senses functioning at incredible rates of speed.

The body helps us to operate in the physical realm by its senses. Its ability to see, taste, touch, hear, and smell allows us to move within a physical universe.

The problem in a Christian is that natural (or secular) man cannot see very far past the realm of his senses. It is true that he wills, he thinks, and he feels—all manifestations of the soul—but he does so with the idea of satisfying the body.

One of the greatest problems Christians face is trying to understand what our physical, carnal, or fleshly nature is and how to find victory over it. Often after a Christian has yielded to the flesh he will excuse himself by saying, "Oh, it's just my old nature acting up." But that can't be since that old nature was crucified with Christ and is now dead (see Rom. 6:6; Gal. 2:20). We must realize that the "flesh" and the old Adamic nature are not the same. They are different, although they work closely together in a non-Christian. (See chapter 5.)

The problem is not the old nature but rather the flesh, which is simply the body and soul cooperating to produce sinful deeds.

But how does "the flesh" manifest itself in a Christian? To answer this we must recognize that the soul stands between the body and the spirit. It stands there with the elements of will, mind, and emotion incorporated into its essence. When these elements cooperate with the body expressing themselves in such a way that they dominate the spirit, sinful flesh is created. Thus we define "sinful flesh"—not sinful nature—as the "cooperation of the soul with the body when they work together to produce actions that displease God." In an unbeliever, the old nature is there to make this happen on a continual basis. But a Christian makes the choice daily either to allow the flesh to reign—producing carnal man—or the spirit to reign—producing spiritual man.

Another thing about our bodies: because of sin, our bodies are in the process of decay and will eventually die. "Man is destined to die once" (Heb. 9:27). This speaks of physical death, or the separation of the soul and spirit from the body. However, a Christian's hope is in resurrection *after* death. The body will be raised at the resurrection. But how can this be?

When the Apostle Paul wrote to the Corinthians, he acknowledged that he was aware that some of them were concerned with how their dead bodies would be raised (1 Cor. 15:35). They could not comprehend rotten, deteriorated flesh and bone becoming a personal body again. In verse 44 Paul explains that the body returns to the ground as a natural body, but when it comes forth again it is a spiritual body. Later he says, "This perishable must clothe itself with the imperishable, and the mortal with immortality" (v. 53).

When Christ came forth from the grave, he came forth in a new glorified body, a body that could apparently appear and disappear at will (John 20:19, 26). And yet his body was a flesh-and-bone body (Luke 24:39) that could be physically touched (v. 27). This same glorified, immortal, incorruptible type of body is what all of God's children will eventually receive: "The Lord Jesus . . . will transform our lowly bodies so that they will be like his glorious body" (Phil. 3:21).

Speaking of dying, the Apostle Paul commented, "I die every day" (1 Cor. 15:31). He, of course, was talking about dying to his own fleshly desires. The choice of dying to sinful deeds is made in our souls. That choice does not obliterate our bodily senses or desires, but rather makes their every move subject to our own spirits when Christ is Lord from within. These senses, then, become subject to righteousness. It is important to understand that we do not have to live frustrated lives by trying to overcome difficulties in our own strength. Christ living within us by his Spirit gives the power to live above sin. If you are struggling over some problem, talk it over with the Lord; ask for his strength to be released in you.

The Soul—Will, Mind, and Emotions. Right now we will simply identify this unique part of man, since we take a more extensive look at the soul's different aspects in another chapter.

As stated before, the soul makes it possible for man to operate in both the natural and spiritual realms. The Hebrew word for soul, *nephesh,* as well as the Greek word, *psuche,* both mean "a breathing creature." God, taking dust and breathing into it the breath of life, made man a living, breathing creature. Job 33:4 says, "The Spirit of God has made me, the breath of the Almighty gives me life." He has "made" us of dust and "breathed" into us spirit which has given us life— soul.

First, notice that the Bible teaches that the *nephesh* is the seat of our wills. Psalm 27:12 says, "Do not turn me over to the desire of my foes." The word used for desire is *nephesh.* The King James Version may make it a little clearer. "Give me not up to the *will* ("nephesh" for soul) of my adversaries" (italics added). These two Scriptures as well as others (eg., Deut. 21:14 and Ps. 35:25) indicate that the soul contains the part of us that makes choices. It is the part where wants and desires accummulate for the purpose of making decisions.

The King James again will help us with this point. "And thou shalt bestow that money for whatever thy soul (nephesh) lusteth (strongly desires) after, for oxen, or for sheep, or for wine, or for strong drink, or for whatsoever thy soul (nephesh) desireth" (Deut. 14:26).

Second, notice that the mind is a part of the soul. The mind is that part of our makeup that stores facts or knowledge and then is later able to recall them from memory and fashion them into conclusions. This is called thinking. "That a soul (nephesh) be without knowledge, it is not good" (Prov. 19:2, KJV). "For as he thinketh in his heart (nephesh) so is he" (Prov. 23:7, KJV). "My soul hath them still in *remembrance*" (Lam. 3:20, KJV; italics added). Other Scriptures to see are Proverbs 2:10 and 24:14.

Third, note that the soul is the seat of our emotions. The term *emotions* usually describes that part of our being where feelings and sensations originate. They may be further described as strong subjective responses. "And David was greatly distressed; for the people spake of stoning him, because the soul of all the people was *grieved* (an emotion)" (1 Sam. 30:6, KJV; italics added). "And the man of God said, 'Let her alone; for her soul is *vexed* (a very strong emotion) within her'" (2 Kings 4:27, KJV; italics added). "Then he said to them, 'My soul is overwhelmed with sorrow to the point of death'" (Matt. 26:38). Here the strong sensation of sorrow captivated the very soul of Jesus himself. In another place John records the impact of strong emotions in the life of Jesus: "Now is my soul troubled" (John 12:27, KJV).

Therefore, while it is true that having a soul indicates that we have natural life, we see further that it is our souls that contain our wills and decisions, our thoughts and reasonings, and our emotions.

The Spirit—Perception, Conviction, Fellowship. The Greek word for spirit is *pneuma*. One of the Greek words for wind is also *pneuma*. Thus wind and spirit came to be associated. Perhaps the ancients thought that spirits were carried on the wind.

The makeup of the spirit is most difficult to describe because we must use the reasoning of the mind—which is in the soul and therefore lower than the spirit—in order to convey its essence. So we are at a major disadvantage to begin with because we are using the soul to understand the spirit. The two realms, although closely related, have important differences. It is only through studying God's Word and becoming attuned to his Spirit that we can recognize and begin to understand and heed the working of our own spirit. It is important that we understand that this life force of spirit is not the uncreated Spirit of God. God has given us our own spirits, but they are created spirits, and therefore different from the eternal Holy Spirit (see Job 33:4).

When Scripture speaks of spiritual death (Eph. 2:1-5) it is not referring to nonexistence. Some assume that the spirit in a person who is outside of Christ is dead in terms of not being there or being dormant. This is incorrect. The spirit of the unregenerated person is very much alive; it is, however, not functioning properly. It is not fulfilling its duty to unite with God in the spiritual realm where Christ is the sum of all things. The Fall of man in the Garden of Eden did not kill the human spirit. However, the spirit *is* dead in the sense that it is not in union with the Author of life.

So, spiritual death is best defined as the spirit's separation from its intended purpose (to glorify God) and its planned destination (eternity with God). Before our spirits can be made alive with Christ (Eph. 3:5) the Holy Spirit must get our attention. Then we are able to perceive with our spirits that we are lost. When we respond to God, the Lord begins to open our hearts through the Word and soon our spirits become active and God raises us up "with Christ" and seats us "in the heavenly realm in Christ Jesus, in order that in the coming ages he might show the incomparable riches of his grace, expressed in his kindness in Christ Jesus" (Eph. 2:6-7). When Christ comes in he moves our spirits towards the fullness of what they were originally created to be. This movement is "rebirth." It literally creates new life (2 Cor. 5:17; Gal. 6:15). Christ did not come to help us become a better people. He came to make us into "new" persons. Thus, the human spirit has the ability to perceive. It is a perception above anything the soul can do. It is the ability to know things intuitively.

Next to perception, the spirit has conviction (or conscience). Conviction for us as believers is the capacity to hear God's warning when we begin to do something wrong. Conviction is aided by a scripturally taught conscience, which makes it easier to hear what the Spirit of God is saying to our human spirits.

Also our spirits contain a very sensitive area designed for communing with God. Unfortunately it is an area most people seldom experience because we are so far departed from God. It is here, in this tender area of our inner being, that we are capable of fellowshiping with God, of entering into his presence.

It should be understood that although the spirit is the element of God-consciousness, it is also the element of demon-consciousness. One of the spiritual gifts is that of discerning spirits (1 Cor. 12:10). Basically, this is the human spirit recognizing and evaluating the presence of other spirits, both human and demonic.

Satan worship, as well as any other form of trafficking in the demonic realm, is done largely through man's spirit. People involved in demon worship have extra-dimensional experiences that are just as real as the experiences Christians have in serving Christ. And because their experiences are so real it is difficult for them to believe they have a spiritual need that can be satisfied only through Jesus Christ (Acts 4:12). To them, their own spiritual reality is truth—regardless of how full of error it may be. And much of what they see, believe, and experience is true. But they do not have the corporate truth found in Jesus Christ. They have found true things in the realm of the one who initially decided to forsake truth. It makes little difference to them that they have entered Satan's territory. It is enough that they have entered a higher reality.

Since the Fall, mankind has clung tenaciously to the soul realm because it is the basic realm, outside of his body, of which he is aware. He would like to believe in a higher realm, but without an experiential understanding he often finds the things of the spirit to be confusing. This confusion exists because the god of this world has blinded the minds of men (2 Cor. 4:4). And even many of those who are born anew in their hearts have not pressed on into a walk in the spirit, but rather carry out most of their Christianity in the soul where it has little benefit or effect.

Because we are separated from God by sin, the human spirit has ceased to commune, to listen, and to perceive God. This nullifies the spirit's basic function and leaves it void of either expression or fulfillment. Hence the idea "dead."

The Fall brought tripart man into disarray. All of his parts are there but they are not cooperating together as God intended. In order to save labor and shipping costs, manufacturers frequently sell their products unassembled. Perhaps nearly as frequently, many of us try to put an item together without reading the instructions. Now, while it is true that God did not create us unassembled, sin has brought about something just as bad: a total confusion of our parts and their functions in relationship to one another. God, therefore, has given us a manual for putting us back together, but it isn't as simple as snapping parts into place. The manual says that each part will need to be refashioned. The body, soul, and spirit—all three— were damaged so severely in the Fall that each must be remanufactured. And this is why Christ has come. The "mystery," Paul says, "is Christ in you, the hope of glory" (Col. 1:27). This indwelling Christ works to make us new creations. But he refuses to work in an individual without that person's consent.

We often use the Scripture verse, "The one who is in you is greater than the one who is in the world" (1 John 4:4), to affirm the fact that we as Christians cannot be overcome by Satan in our spirits. That is well and good. But why not go a step further and use the same verse to affirm that we do not need to be overcome in the areas of body and soul either? With the Spirit of Christ not only being "with" us but "in" us (John 14:17), there comes change—complete change. "If anyone is in Christ, he is a new creation" (2 Cor. 5:17).

And that change will likewise affect all the areas of our being, especially our souls—as we shall discover.

NOTES

1. David Watson, *The Hidden Battle: Strategies for Spiritual Victory* (Wheaton: Harold Shaw Publishers, 1980), 64.
2. Charles R. Swindoll, *Dropping Your Guard* (Waco, TX: Word Books, 1983), 128-129.
3. It is appropriate here to mention that some dichotomists' (those who see man as a two-part being—body and soul) points of view sustain some validity. Charles Hodge in *Systematic Theology* argues that the soul and the spirit are different forms of the same substance. This point I will not argue. If he sees the body as the tangible substance (outer man) and the soul and spirit as the intangible substance (inner man) there is some basis for agreement. But I wholeheartedly maintain that within that intangible substance there exist two distinct entities, soul and spirit.

Hodge further argues that "no man is conscious . . . of the soul as different from the spirit." I do not agree. There is a definite conscious difference between the two, a recognizable difference when the elements of each is defined (see chapter 3).

Please note that I use a tripart explanation of man more as a model for illustration than a strict unbending theological point of view. I'm sure our makeup has much more to it that only eternity will reveal.

FOUR

Overcoming in the
Soul Realm

When Jesus sent out the Twelve to preach "to the lost sheep of Israel," he told them to not "be afraid of those who kill the body but cannot kill the soul. Rather, be afraid of the one who can destroy both soul and body in hell" (Matt. 10:28). Since God holds the direction of an individual's eternal future in light of that person's response to the Cross, the enemy does everything possible to keep men from surrendering to Christ.

The struggle to do good or evil, to be saved or lost, is waged in the soul—the place where each person must decide and choose. It is there that we think and reason, that we have feeling and learn to express ourselves. Satan, through his demonic forces, attacks our wills, our minds, and our emotions—the three primary elements of the soul. For he knows that if he can get us to succumb to sin and keep us wrapped up in it so that we never come to know Christ, he has destroyed us for eternity. This is his goal, to prevent the love of God from entering the human heart (see John 10:10).

Although demons are responsible for much of the confusion that exists in our souls, they cannot, as we stated earlier, always be blamed for all of our prob-

73

lems. Our own sin and the resulting separation from God also account for much of our behavior.

Outside of Christ, we face the problems of sin on the one hand and a slave master (Satan) on the other. This makes it impossible to have inner peace. And contrary to what we may think when we first come to Christ, we are not excluded from the war. We still face struggles of many kinds. But now our battles are somewhat different. God's Holy Spirit encourages us to contend with the inordinate appetites of our bodies and to do warfare against oppressing demon spirits. Neither of these areas of contention, however, need cause us defeat or lack of continued peace. When Christ is living in our spirits he helps us keep our bodies in control, and Christ within also gives us power to overcome the enemy (1 John 4:4).

Look with me for a moment at the evidence of battles taking place within the three parts of the soul— the will, the mind, and the emotions. Many people face an inner battle when first confronted with the claims of the gospel. Some unbelievers will wrestle, sometimes for years, in their *wills*, deciding whether or not they will accept Christ. Their *minds* are bombarded with all kinds of questions as to the validity of the message. Their *emotions* move them to fear and they become afraid that following Christ will cost too much.

These people often attack what they think are inconsistencies in the lives of Christians. This, they believe, excuses them from making commitments for themselves. Often they make attempts to do good, but they fail consistently. Then their minds tell them that if they become Christians it will be necessary to try even harder. All of their past failures suggest to them only more failure. Their minds, wrapped up in their emotions, keep their wills from making the proper choice concerning Christ. And the battle rages on.

If it were not for the love of God, that inner resistance to the call of our Savior would never be broken down. But God can be praised, for even when demons are directly involved, love—God's unconditional *agape* love—comes as a powerful force to break our rebellion against our Creator.

THE WILL

We make our decisions in our wills. That is where we find the prerogative to choose. God created us with free will, so we are capable of making choices. And this is what God wants. Yet he wants it within the confines of universal law—a law set up to protect, and not to hinder, inner volition. Satan moves by coercion, but God moves by persuasion; he never intended for us to be robots.

This same *will* (as well as mind and emotions, the two other aspects of our soul) faces a battlefront: We must decide either to submit to God or to join the rebellion. Then we must choose between living in spirit with the Holy Spirit or walking after the flesh. As the inner debate takes place, our minds interject thoughts either affirming or denying the pending decision. Emotions such as love, hate, fear, and sorrow also help our wills to choose.

The personal internal battle between flesh and spirit is waged not because our bodily needs have no right to fulfillment, because they most assuredly do. Rather, the battle is fought because those needs want to dominate, which they should not. Unless the bodily senses and needs are submitted to the soul and spirit, they will always produce unrighteousness. When the soul gives in to the body's unrestrained appetites we commonly refer to the results as *fleshly* or *carnal* actions (Rom. 7:14; 1 Cor. 3:1-3, KJV) or, as the New International Version says, "unspiritual" or "worldly" actions. It is at this point that the self-life emerges.

With self in control we are not the person God created us to be. But it need not be that way. It is possible that our whole being can be put right again, with the spirit ruling the soul and body. Any attempt to change, however, without the supernatural power of the Holy Spirit is met with intense resistance from our flesh. If you have ever tried to go on a diet, quit smoking, stop drinking, refrain from taking narcotics, or quit some powerful habit, then you know what I mean. Outside of Christ the body's senses with the soul's carnal desires are so powerful and dictatorial that they put up a tremendous battle when they are denied in the slightest way. We need help to put the body as well as the soul back in their rightful places. To do so, we need God's help; we will never be completely whole or right without our Creator.

From the cradle to the grave our focus is on "me." But that "me" is not the real *me*. It is a "me" generated by a cooperation between the soul and the body, rather than one generated by a cooperation between soul and *spirit*. When this first "me" rules, it creates the self-life.

Many times those who try to point out the error of this self-oriented life-style say one must be "crucified" with Christ (Rom. 6:6) in order to become a whole person. While that is true, people often confuse the initial crucifixion of the old nature, which takes place at conversion, with the need for daily sanctification. (*Sanctification* means to be set apart for the Lord.)

The old nature was crucified when we were born again. Now we must deal with flesh. But crucifixion of "self" is not annihilation of the real you. The terms *crucifixion of self, self-denial,* and *dying to self* all indicate our need to move away from bondage to the body—where we are out of control—toward the realm where our regenerated spirits are in control. But this is not possible until the old, Adamic nature has been done away with in Christ. (See chapter 5.) The spirit cannot be in control, as God intended it to be at creation, until Christ enters in to give it stability. We were not made to live without a vibrant personal relationship with our Creator. Augustine said it well, "Thou hast formed us for thyself, and our hearts are restless till they find rest in thee."

And yet in our own fallen condition we are constantly demanding our rights. We insist on being the "gods" of our own destiny. Oswald Chambers says:

> The Bible does not say that God punished the human race for one man's sin; but that the disposition of sin, viz., my claim to my right to myself, entered into the human race by one man, and that another Man took on Him the sin of the human race and put it away (Heb. 9:26)—an infinitely profounder revelation. The disposition of sin is not immorality and wrongdoing, but the disposition of self-realization—I am my own god.[1]

Those who live the self-life outside of God believe they are living in maximum freedom. To them, the righteous life is one of puritanical rules and restraints that will keep them from being free. But we who are in Christ know that just the opposite is true. For, as James Hefley notes, "When people cease to be good, they soon cease to be free."

A man who has a perfectly obedient dog takes him with him wherever he goes. Another man has a dog he can't trust and therefore must keep chained most of the time. Which is most free, the independent dog who must be tethered or the perfectly obedient dog?

As the "free" man basks in what he thinks is freedom he becomes increasingly bound. He truly believes that he can practice the sins of his self-life, laying them aside whenever he chooses. He does not understand the bondage that comes from feeding self. When

all too soon he experiences its effects, he seldom corre-
lates his problems with his life-style. He may soon
hate himself. He may begin to see no hope in his life as
he develops an *Is-this-all-there-is?* attitude. He doesn't
know that the distasteful element of self can be
changed with the help of Jesus Christ. Leighton Ford
says, "Absolute freedom is absolute nonsense. There is
no such thing. Freedom finds fulfillment only within
its limitation. A train is designed to run freely on the
rails. A fish is designed to live freely in the water. A
basketball player or hockey player is free to use his
skills only within the rules. And get this: A human
being is designed to be truly, genuinely human, only in
a relationship to God, our Creator."

But living the self-life is not confined to non-Chris-
tians. Born-again believers often find themselves
trapped in a humanistic self-centered existence. The
Apostle Paul warned the saints at Colosse to "put to
death, therefore, whatever belongs to your earthly nature: sexual immorality, impurity, lust, evil desires and
greed, which is idolatry. . . . You used to walk in these
ways, in the life you once lived. But now you must rid
yourselves of all such things as these: anger, rage, mal-
ice, slander, and filthy language from your lips" (Col.
3:5,7).

How does a person break these bonds of self-living?
Prayer is the Christian's solution to these problems.
E. Herman writes, "It is upon our willingness to listen
and hear God speak that our prayer life from first to
last depends. This should be clear when we remember
that prayer is the soul's pilgrimage from self to God;
and the most effectual remedy for self-love and self-
absorption is the habit of humble listening."[2] (We say
much more about this solution in the final chapter of
this book.)

Even after Christ enters our spirits we must exercise
our own wills on a daily basis to live outside the flesh-

ly, sinful desires of body and soul. As we learn to abide in Christ our spirits stay in control. *Abide* means to settle down to stay. Righteousness is incorporated into our life-style. Now communion with God takes place; there is a settling and a true inner peace because we function as God originally created us to function. Of course we will still have problems; the complete redemption of body and soul has yet to take place. But for now, as "abiding" children of God, we are where God wants us to be. We are on our way to becoming overcomers.

When we understand what the self-life is and recognize that it has no benefits and nothing desirable, when we understand that this present life is not all there is nor will be, but that God is preparing for himself a people destined for a realm that is indescribable, then it is easier to see what Christ meant when he said, "For whoever wants to save his life will lose it; but whoever loses his life for me will find it" (Matt. 16:25). He wasn't talking about lying down and physically dying because the next life is better than this one. He wasn't talking about asceticism (self-crucifixion) where a man tortures himself to get God's attention or to atone for his sins. He was talking about letting the carnal interests of the self-life die—those interests which come about when the body and soul cooperate to the exclusion of the spirit. He was talking about destroying the goals of this temporal life, goals that are not submitted to the purposes of the eternal.

"What good will it be for a man if he gains the whole world, yet forfeits his soul? Or what can a man give in exchange for his soul?" (Matt. 16:26). What does a man gain if his will, mind, and emotions fail to take on spiritual life in Christ? What profit is there to receiving the world if the elements of the soul are too destitute to rule it? What advantage is there to allowing sin and Satan the right to rule?

And so in order to keep the soul from ruin, Christ said, "If anyone would come after me, he must deny himself and take up his cross and follow me" (Matt. 16:24). The Apostle Paul said that "we have been united with [Christ] in his death" (Rom. 6:5). We died to our old nature with him on the cross. Now we must die daily to sinful deeds. This is not a negative aspect of Christianity. It is very positive. Dying to that which is no good will not hurt anyone. Paul said he bore the "death of Jesus, so that the life of Jesus may also be revealed" in his body (2 Cor. 4:10).

We die to the flesh that we might have life in Christ. We die to that which is old that we might attain that which is new. We die to self so that the real person inside might come forth. "Jesus said to her, 'I am the resurrection and the life. He who believes in me will live, even though he dies; and whoever lives and believes in me will never die' " (John 11:25-26). When we die to sin and self, we appear to the world to be foolish. Our refusal to participate in worldly activities brings criticism and sneering. But we actually die to that which is producing death, for Christ has guaranteed that "death" to self brings eternal life.

Paul stated, "I die every day" (1 Cor. 15:31). As an act of his will he continually died to the desires of his body, desires that would hinder spiritual life. "In the same way, count yourselves dead to sin but alive to God in Christ Jesus. Therefore, *do not let* sin reign in your mortal body so that you obey its evil desires" (Rom. 6:11-12, italics added).

No doubt, Paul ate, drank, laughed, and enjoyed life as much as one can enjoy anything in the midst of battle. Paul was not morbid about living, he simply knew that what the world saw as life was really death. And so to receive "the crown that will last forever" (1 Cor. 9:25), Paul cooperated with God. But his life-style would never be received by the world, for those without God's Spirit cannot accept the things that come from God's Spirit; they consider these things to be foolishness, they cannot understand them because they are discerned spiritually (see 1 Cor. 2:14). Paul's cooperation with God led him to say, "I have been crucified with Christ and I no longer live, but Christ lives in me. The life I live in the body, I live by faith in the Son of God, who loved me and gave himself for me" (Gal. 2:20).

If we are to be overcomers we must walk with Christ; all stubbornness in our wills must be rejected. Such rejection puts the higher person, the person God originally intended us to be when he created humanity, in control.

Relationships will at times gender strife, bitterness, and hatred, so they must be met with the love of God. We do this with God's help simply by crushing the stubbornness and rebellion that desperately try to manifest themselves, then allowing the sweetness of Christ to come forth. By yielding directly to Christ during difficult situations we can literally take command of ourselves in the will and live in righteousness. When temptation comes, yielding to Christ and resisting temptation become acts of our wills. The more we exercise the will this way, the stronger the true essence of it becomes.

Note here that it is very important to realize that self-effort will never overcome the self-life. Self-effort is a vain attempt to pull ourselves up by our own boot straps. We need God's help; he alone can release us from the foolishness and bondage of self. A. W. Tozer said, "Self is the opaque veil that hides the face of God from us. It can be removed only in spiritual experience, never by mere instruction. We may as well try to instruct leprosy out of our system. *There must be a work of God in destruction before we are free*" (italics mine).[3]

Those outside of Christ desperately want to express their wills. They want to feel the freedom of individuality, the expression of the person God created each of them to be. But frequently infectious demon spirits are at the root of many of their decisions. So it is not really *their* wills they are exercising, but rather the wills of demons.

The human will must never be taken lightly. It must be recognized as the manifestation of the persons we are and intend to become. And it must be changed where it is wrong.

THE MIND

The mind is the term we use to indicate the inner place where thoughts, intellect, reason, understanding, and remembering take place. The brain is the physiological place where the mind operates.

It is in our minds that most spiritual warfare takes place. As we will see later, Satan works on our emotions—hatred, despondency, despair, depression, worry, fear, resentment, jealousy, wrath—using them to affect the mind. He then continues to work there in order to get to our wills, for once the enemy has a person's will he has most of the control he needs to accomplish his purposes. But for maximum control, his goal is to get to the human spirit. Thus Satan works hard on our thought-life.

When we are born again, the Spirit of Jesus is allowed direct and immediate entrance to our spirits, where he desires to do all of his communication with us. When Christ speaks to our spirits, they eventually communicate the message to our minds and we are able to understand and carry out God's directive. Suddenly we understand what our spirits see.

One reason so many Christians have trouble listening to God is that their minds are not fixed on the things of God. One minute their thoughts are on him, the next on the world, and the next on the flesh. Soon they are angry with God because he never seems to answer their prayers. They would receive more answers if they would learn to listen in their spirits. But this takes time, for only time spent alone in the presence of God will allow him to communicate to the human spirit.

Because of this, Satan's work almost always starts in the mind, where he implants his doctrines, and where we are tempted. Then, once he takes control of the mind, he reaches out to the other areas of body and spirit.

Christ also works first in the mind. Our initial response to repent takes place here. Repentance actually means "to change one's mind." With our cooperation, God enters the human spirit through the mind. Once this takes place, new life, spiritual life in Jesus Christ, begins. We become "a new creation" (2 Cor. 5:17) and reflect almost immediate change even though it may seem very small at first. Love replaces hate. Joy replaces sadness. Peace replaces fear. But if our minds are not renewed daily through God's Word and prayer, it is possible to have a good heart and a bad head. In other words, we can have hearts that want righteousness and affirm the goodness of God, but heads filled with everything from questionable doctrines to pharisaical legalisms. Our minds can become confused soon after we receive our salvation; fear, doubt, worry, and anxiety all return to try to destroy the inner peace of our salvation. Our spirits become alive toward God but our minds remain unrenewed. This is why we are told in Romans 12:2 to "be transformed by the renewing of your mind" (see also Eph. 4:22-24). We put on this new mind by an act of our will.

With Christ living within us it would seem that we should have very little trouble with sin or Satan. But

83

this is not always true because of the condition of our minds. Isaiah sang, "You [God] will keep him in perfect peace whose mind is steadfast, because he trusts in you" (26:3). We must continually trust in the Lord with steadfast minds, or else our minds will tend toward the body and sin, and be ground for enemy attack.

The mind, then, becomes vulnerable to attacks by the enemy for two reasons: first, because it is not being renewed in Christ, and second, because it is not steadfast, trusting in him. In these situations the mind can become the playground of the enemy.

> If we carefully examine the mental experiences of a Christian we shall see that not merely is he narrow-minded but that he contains many other defects too. His head, for instance, may be teeming with all kinds of uncontrollable thoughts, imaginations, impure pictures, wanderings and confused ideas. His memory may suddenly fail; his power of concentration may be weakened; he may be obsessed by prejudices which arise from unknown sources; his thoughts may be retarded as if his mind were being chained; or he may be flushed with wild thoughts which revolve unceasingly in his head. The Christian may find he is powerless to regulate his mental life and make it obey the intent of his will. He forgets innumerable matters both large and small. He carries out many improper actions, without knowing why and without so much as investigating the reason. Physically he is quite healthy, but mentally he does not comprehend the explanation for these symptoms. Currently many saints encounter these mental difficulties, but without ever knowing why.[4]

If, occasionally (or consistently), this is our experience, we can be sure that God is not in total control, because such thoughts don't come from him. And if these are thoughts we do not want, then we aren't in control either. Therefore, we must conclude that (aside from some physical malady) they are satanic in origin. But God has granted us free will and he wants us to be in control of our entire being, including our minds. In order to stay in control of ourselves we have to daily renew our minds, thinking the things of God (see Phil. 4:8) so that the Holy Spirit can give us the power to stay in control.

Satan often uses our memories of things to hold us in bondage. He flashes pictures in our minds which in turn excite our bodies. In this way demon spirits work at getting us to succumb to the flesh. Often these spirits will tip their hand by planting foreign thoughts, thoughts that do not come from our memories because we have never seen or experienced what we are thinking. Rather they are brought by the demons involved. Many ungodly writings and works of art have come about by such direct satanic inspiration.

A mind that won't shut off and a mind that won't switch on are frequently the results of demonic activity. At times these demons work to force the mind to think excessively, and at other times they try to render it incapable of sound mental activity.

Scripture speaks of the mind in many different ways: sinful-natured (Rom. 8:5-6); unscriptural (Col. 2:18); corrupt (Titus 1:15); depraved (Rom. 1:28); double (James 1:8; 4:8); futile (Eph. 4:17); worried (Luke 12:29); deceived and led astray (2 Cor. 11:3); and poisoned (Acts 14:2). All these mental attitudes need renewal. When a mind is in tune with God it becomes humble (Acts 20:19; Col. 3:12); willing (2 Cor. 8:12); self-disciplined (2 Tim. 1:7); eager (Acts 17:11); and wholesome (2 Pet. 3:1).

Sometimes Christians, in seeking fellowship with God, allow their minds to become passive. Their sincere desire to hear from God, especially in prayer, causes them to open their thought-life to whatever comes in, thinking that only God will speak to them.

Blanking out all thoughts as much as possible, they assume they are now ready to hear from the Lord. They do not understand that God speaks to our spirits, and our spirits then communicate to our minds—and that all of this is in accord with the written Word. For the Spirit and the Word must agree.

To leave our minds wide open, without questioning and discerning the source of input, advances Satan's purposes. We can become confused when our spirits caution us, but our minds speak so loudly against that caution that we feel guilty if we do not obey.

Demons often apply a mental force that is much different from the gentle constraint of the Holy Spirit when he gives direction. This powerful coercion from the enemy commands us to carry out an order without question. God's admonition to "try the spirits" (1 John 4:1) is seldom beneficial at this point, for any questioning seems to be disobedience. Such demons usually apply additional pressure by instilling the thought that the matter must be accomplished in haste: "Don't ask questions, just hurry." And so, if we are not aware of the enemy's devices, we scurry about until we are spiritually, mentally, and physically worn out—which is exactly what Satan wants (see Dan. 7:25).

At times, believers fall prey to what appear to be "good" thoughts, thoughts that seem religious and right. Because these thoughts seem good, there is never the inclination to question them. But because they were not born in the spirit by the Holy Spirit they will never bear fruit. Many Christians with good hearts fall for the lies of these "spirits of religion" and their efforts have little effect on furthering the kingdom of God. They constantly keep busy doing good deeds but their motivation is not from God's Word or his Spirit.

Mature Christians are careful when they use the expression "God told me." They understand that whatever they hear must be carefully confirmed by God's

Word as well as by other mature Christians. The Holy Spirit living in others will confirm the direction that God gives. It is the Holy Spirit in others that bears witness with our spirit, either confirming or denying the input.

It is extremely important to test every theory and determine the source of every thought. Failure to discover the origin of what we hear or read provides the enemy with a place to work.

God's Word cautions us against deception: "Then we will no longer be infants, tossed back and forth by waves, and blown here and there by every wind of teaching and by the cunning and craftiness of men in their deceitful scheming" (Eph. 4:14); "The Spirit clearly says that in later times some will abandon the faith and follow deceiving spirits and things taught by demons" (1 Tim. 4:1); "For such men are false apostles, deceitful workmen, masquerading as apostles of Christ. And no wonder, for Satan himself masquerades as an angel of light. It is not surprising, then, if his servants masquerade as servants of righteousness. Their end will be what their actions deserve" (2 Cor. 11:13-15); "I am astonished that you are so quickly deserting the one who called you by the grace of Christ and are turning to a different gospel—which is really no gospel at all. Evidently some people are throwing you into confusion and are trying to pervert the gospel of Christ. But even if we or an angel from heaven should preach a gospel other than the one we preached to you, let him be eternally condemned!" (Gal. 1:6-8). "Watch out for false prophets. They come to you in sheep's clothing, but inwardly they are ferocious wolves. By their fruit you will recognize them" (Matt. 7:15-17). And finally, Paul says to Timothy: "Preach the word; be prepared in season and out of season; correct, rebuke and encourage—with great patience and careful instruction. For the time will come when men will not put up with sound doctrine. Instead, to suit their own desires, they will gather around them a great number of teachers to say what their itching ears want to hear. They turn their ears away from the truth and turn aside to myths" (2 Tim. 4:2-4). (Recommended reading: *Unholy Devotion* by Harold Bazell, Zondervan Publishing House.)

THE EMOTIONS

Again, man's mind was given to him that he might think and reason, his will that he might choose and decide, and his emotions that he might express his feelings.

Our emotions are perhaps our most complex and least understood aspect. We go from joy to sorrow, happiness to sadness, and peace to anxiety—all in a matter of moments. We are never quite sure why we feel one way or another. And worse yet, we never take the time to explore the reasons for our feelings.

Emotions, for the most part, issue from the soul. They give expression to personality and should describe what is happening in our spirits. They should never control us. But now they tend to control much of our being. They work hard to influence the mind and ultimately the will. As the spirit was ordained to be in control of the soul and the soul to control the body, similarly the will was to control the mind and the mind to control the emotions. But the Fall flipped things upside down and now the emotions control the mind, and the mind controls the will. And these emotions take their cues from the senses in the body, thus allowing the body unlawful control. This governorship from unrestrained emotions is the source of many, if not most, of the problems we face.

In light of this, we can better understand, and deal

with, a strong foe: temptation. "The cravings of sinful man, the lust of the eyes and the boasting of what he has and does" (1 John 2:16) work in a particular way. When the body senses—sight, touch, taste, etc.—are not controlled by the spirit, they begin to dictate, telling the soul what to do and be. The soul then dictates to the emotions, which dictate to the mind, which dictates to the will. And so we find ourselves saying, "The things I want to do, I can't. The things I don't want to do, I always find myself doing." We would like to do good, but somehow we can't find the power to do it. And eventually temptation turns to sin.

We are inclined to look at emotions and label them as either good or bad. For example, happiness would be good while sadness would be bad. But the basic problem is not one of good or bad emotions; rather it is that emotions tend to control illegitimately. Whereas they were meant to be submissive to the will and the mind, this is not now the case for fallen humanity and, sad to say, for many Christians.

Emotions can be erratic. All too frequently we allow their highs and lows to rule the rest of our being. At times, even though our minds would like to reason the truth or fallacy of a particular point and the will would like to choose according to biblical principles, the emotions demand control and we end up in a carnal condition.

If we have trouble walking in the spirit, it could well be that we do not understand the role of our emotions. Some believe that a high emotional state indicates a high spiritual level; others believe that a deeply spiritual person is melancholy and passive. Both views are subject to problems, for in both cases the emotions are still in control. Only when we move into the realm of the spirit will we discover that neither high emotions nor suppressed emotions indicate how spiritual we are. Rather our spirituality is determined by our communion with God in the Holy of Holies—our spirits.

Emotions have far less a place in our spiritual lives than most of us want to believe. If we are going to mature, they must take a backseat to the will and the mind, which in turn must submit to the spirit. We might go one step further and suggest that until the emotions are almost silenced it will be virtually impossible for our spirits to hear the quiet yet distinct voice of the Holy Spirit. When God's Word says, "My God shall supply all your needs" (Phil. 4:19), the soul argues the point, usually at the bidding of the emotions. Fear then causes doubt; anxiety soon damages patience; and the flesh gains control—all because we did not follow the leading of the spirit. "Be it therefore recognized that when the spirit ceases to lead, emotion will do so. During such a period the believer will interpret emotional impulses to be motions of inspirations. An emotional Christian can be compared to a pond of sand and mud: as long as no one disturbs the water the pond looks clear and clean; but let it be agitated a moment and its true muddy character appears."[5]

One reason many Christians are ineffective as soldiers of the Cross is that they are overly influenced by emotions. Their spirituality is worn like a hat. They put it on one minute and take it off the next, all depending on how they feel. But emotions were never meant to control, rule, or govern our existence. When we allow them to do so they rob us of spiritual power. A Christian must understand that God desires to work through his *spirit*, not his soul, and thus not through his emotions.

This is not to say that we cannot or should not express emotions. But the higher working of the spirit must be in control at all times to make emotions the expressions of the spirit in tune with the Holy Spirit,

not of carnality and sin. Note again the words of
Watchman Nee:

> If [the Christian] in fact acknowledges that no life of
> God resides in his emotion, he will never attempt to
> secure the salvation of people by means of his power
> of emotion through tears, mournful face, cries, or other
> emotional devices. No effort of his emotion can affect
> in the slightest the darkened human spirit. Except the
> Holy Spirit gives life, man can have no life. If we do not
> rely on the Spirit and use emotion instead, our work
> will yield no real fruit.
>
> Those who labor for the Lord need to see distinctly
> that nothing in man can generate God's life. We may
> exhaust every psychological method to excite man's
> emotion, to arouse his interest in religion, to make him
> sorry and shameful for his past history, to create in
> him a fear of the coming penalty, to foster admiration
> of Christ, to induce him to seek communication with
> Christians, or to be merciful to the poor: we may even
> cause him to feel happy in doing these things: but we
> cannot regenerate him. Since interest, sorrow, shame,
> fear, admiration, aspiration, pity and joy are merely
> various impulses of emotion, man can experience all
> these and his spirit still be dead for he has not yet
> apprehended God intuitively.[6]

When the Holy Spirit works in our spirits to convict
us of sin we will often show some emotion. The same is
true when deliverance takes place. Should we deny
this emotion? Not necessarily. But we must never allow
emotions to overshadow the communication and conviction that is coming from the Lord. If the Holy Spirit
moves upon us profoundly and we let emotions—even
good ones such as joy—so overwhelm what God is
trying to say that the message is lost, then we miss
God.

Without a doubt God wants us to feel good. But feelings of true well-being come to us only from the changes that Christ brings within us as he establishes inner righteousness.

We must take our emotions to the Cross, as we must do with any matter that is not in accordance with God's design. Until our emotions are submitted to our spirits, we will never experience the wonder and beauty of a gentle walk in the Holy Spirit.

NOTES

1. Oswald Chambers, *My Utmost for His Highest* (New York: Dodd, Mead, and Company, 1935), 279.
2. E. Herman, *Creative Prayer* (Cincinnati, Ohio: Forward Movement Publications), 24-25.
3. A. W. Tozer, *The Pursuit of God* (Harrisburg, Penn.: Christian Publications, 1982), 46.
4. Watchman Nee, *The Spiritual Man* (New York: Christian Fellowship Publications, 1968), vol. 3, 13-14.
5. Ibid., 2:192.
6. Ibid., 197.

FIVE

Overcoming in the World

It is said that while John Wesley was preaching on avoiding the things of the world, someone yelled out, "Wesley, what do you mean 'the world'?" The evangelist responded instantly, "Anything that cools my affection for Jesus Christ is the world."[1]

The Book of Common Prayer states: "Lord, we beseech thee, grant thy people grace to withstand the temptation of the world, the flesh, and the devil, and with pure hearts and minds follow thee the only God; through Jesus Christ our Lord."

The enemies, then, that would deter us from "pure hearts and minds" are the *world*, the *flesh*, and the *devil*. These are the forces that must be overcome as we follow "the only God; through Jesus Christ our Lord."

OVERCOMING THE WORLD
The Satanic Federation. On the night of his betrayal and arrest, Jesus prayed to God about his followers. He said, "I have given them your word and the world has hated them, for they are not of the world any more

than I am of the world" (John 17:14). Paul, in Romans 12:2, told the church, "Do not conform any longer to the pattern of this world, but be transformed by the renewing of your mind." This "world" to which we are not to conform is not to be confused with the physical planet earth or with the inhabitants of the earth. John 3:16 tells us that God loves the world—the people who dwell here.

Neither does "the world" refer to the age or time span in which we live. Rather, the "world" that Jesus and Paul warn against is that which makes up this planet's social system, that which incorporates all of man's beliefs and the expressions of those beliefs. This world involves art, music, politics, spiritual matters, science, philosophy and all other aspects of life that are contrived without God's input.

Our minds are capable of tremendous creativity and reason. However, outside of God, all our plans and reasonings have done nothing but lead us into trouble. Nevertheless, we continue to create, to reason, and to think independently of him, disregarding his plans and guidelines. These endeavors, although they may seem good, appropriate, and worthwhile on the surface, are at enmity with God because they are not in accord with his plans. And it is these things that form the world system spoken of in John and Romans.

This is not to say that everything that godless men do in their ignorance of God and in the deception of the enemy should be shunned. Men who do not know God work farms, build automobiles, design homes, construct roads, discover vaccines to cure diseases, and much more—all of which can be beneficial. Many ungodly people sincerely desire to do good and want to see peace on earth. I do not use the word *ungodly* to refer to man's desire for either good or evil. Rather, I use it to refer to the placement of a person's allegiance. Either one knows God and knows that he knows him because of his faith in Jesus Christ, or he follows the "prince of this world" (John 14:30). We either consciously follow God through Christ—or we follow after the rebellion, knowingly or unknowingly.

Furthermore, by calling the people of the world "ungodly," I do not mean to cast aspersions on them, implying that they are inferior to or more sinful than those who know God. Even those who know God still have trouble with sin (1 John 1:8-9). However, the ungodly have not made God the prime mover in their lives. They continue to follow the world's system. A person aligned with God through Jesus Christ has laid down his rebellion; the ungodly are still a part of the resistance. When a person is aligned with God, he has already passed from death to life and has a clearer understanding of who he is, why he is here, and where he is going. Those who are not submitted to God are open to all manner of satanic confusion. Daily they are confronted by peace movements, social concerns, prejudices, evolution, philosophy, world hunger, and a thousand other problems for which they try to figure out solutions without God's help. With all of this thinking, planning, desiring, reasoning, and creating, these people weave a system opposed to God. They become "friend[s] of the world" (James 4:4).

Just what does the world system believe? A good cross section of this system today is expressed in humanistic philosophy. In Humanist Manifestos I and II we find the core of the satanic inspired mind-set of the world:

> We find insufficient evidence for belief in the existence of a supernatural; it is either meaningless or irrelevant to the question of the survival and fulfillment of the human race. . . . We can discover no divine purpose or providence for the human species. . . . No deity will save us; we must save ourselves. . . . Science affirms

that the human species is an emergence from natural evolutionary forces. As far as we know, the total personality is a function of the biological organism transacting in a social and cultural context. There is no credible evidence that life survives the death of the body. . . . We affirm that moral values derive their source from human experience. Ethics is autonomous and situational, needing no theological or ideological sanction. Ethics stems from human need and interest. . . . In the area of sexuality, we believe that intolerant attitudes, often cultivated by orthodox religions and puritanical cultures, unduly repress sexual conduct. The right to birth control, abortion, and divorce should be recognized. . . . The many varieties of sexual exploration should not in themselves be considered "evil." Without countenancing mindless permissiveness or unbridled promiscuity, a civilized society should be a tolerant one. . . . Individuals should be permitted to express their sexual proclivities and pursue their lifestyles as they desire. . . . Moral education for children and adults is an important way of developing awareness and sexual maturity.[2]

This world system cannot and must never be regarded as neutral. It is not a part of that over which God exercises control. Therefore it is energized by the power of Satan. This is true of all who are unsaved. Satan's demons work in some way to affect all of those who are disobedient. "As for you, you were dead in your transgressions and sins, in which you used to live when you followed the ways of this world and of the ruler of the kingdom of the air, *the spirit who is now at work in those who are disobedient*" (Eph. 2:1-2, italics added). Anyone unsaved is under the power of darkness. "We know that we are children of God, and that the whole world is under the control of the evil one" (1 John 5:19).

In 2 Corinthians 4:3-4, Satan is said to cause spiritual blindness in those who do not believe so that the glorious gospel will remain hidden from them. Ephesians 4:18 talks further of the "blindness of their heart." The only way, then, to escape this system is to be purged and cleansed from its influences by the Word of God and by a dynamic spiritual relationship with Jesus Christ. He told us, "In this world you will have trouble. But take heart! I have overcome the world" (John 16:33).

The influences of the world system are extremely subtle. Although people are warned against its effects, they often find themselves deeply confused because many who are in this system are "nice, loving, caring, and concerned individuals." And so they conclude it must be a good system. Ironically, most people involved in the world system are not even aware that it is in opposition to God. They are blind to a war in which their eternal lives are at stake.

For more information about this system read the following passages: Matthew 16:26; John 5:4; John 14:30; James 1:27; James 4:4; 2 Peter 1:4; 2 Peter 2:20.

OVERCOMING THE FLESH

Earlier we talked about the relationship of the body, the soul, and the spirit. In order to understand better what we mean by "the flesh," we want to take another look at our total makeup. As we said before, when God created Adam and Eve he apparently planned that the spirit would control the soul and the soul would control the body. When Adam and Eve fell, this unique relationship was disturbed. Instead of the spirit being dominant, the body assumed the place of authority. The body[3] now rules the soul and the soul now rules the spirit. When the spirit was in control before the Fall, the body was not subject to sin. When man broke fellowship with God, the body took control and subsequently was overcome by the power of sin. This simple illustration is not meant to be a strict theological treatise but is designed as help in understanding why we often feel "pulled" in different directions.

Paul the apostle spoke of the resulting dilemma in Romans 7:18-19: "I have the desire to do what is good, but I cannot carry it out. For what I do is not the good I want to do; no, the evil I do not want to do—this I keep on doing." Paul was acknowledging that the soul stands between what we know to be right and what the senses in our bodies keep telling us to do, and that here in this middle ground he felt a strong pull from opposite sides. When man is out of fellowship with God, the soul stands there trying to figure out which way to go—and usually ends up going in the wrong direction because it is so used to cooperating with the body under the influence of the old nature.

Paul went on to say that he didn't do wrong himself but, rather, "sin living in me does it" (v. 20), forcing him into bondage. His inner struggle prevented him from doing the good which he desired. We often face this same inner struggle—two forces pulling in two different directions. And although it seems logical to blame sin for our problems, God still holds us responsible for the actions produced by that sin. "The soul who sins is the one who will die" (Ezek. 18:20).

At the end of Romans 7 it almost appears that Paul is saying that since the body is so strong, he should go ahead and let it do what it wants to do and just obey his spirit with his mind, not his body. But this is not so. The body and the spirit cannot both be in control. One or the other must govern. Paul exhorts us to "put aside the deeds of darkness and put on the armor of light. Let us behave decently as in the daytime, not in orgies and drunkenness, not in sexual immorality and debauchery, not in dissension and jealousy. Rather, clothe yourselves with the Lord Jesus Christ, and do not think about how to gratify the desires of the flesh" (Rom. 13:12-14). The solution to allowing the spirit to control and to putting aside the evil deeds produced by unrestrained body senses (flesh) is found only in Jesus Christ. Christ's Spirit, living and dwelling in us, turns us upside down—or, really, right-side-up—until spirit controls soul and soul controls body. Old things (including our old Adamic nature) pass away and all things become new (2 Cor. 5:17). The spirit once again becomes dominant as it was before Adam and Eve sinned, and once again comes into a position for communication with God's Spirit.

We may decide, in our souls, to let our spirits be in control rather than the body senses. But without help we will not have sufficient power to carry out that desire. We need Christ to accomplish that. When Christ comes in he does not want to dominate us in the sense of removing our free will. He wants to establish control in our spirits so that we have power and knowledge to make correct choices through our souls. This is why Paul's teaching on "Christ in you" is so important. Christ's Spirit moves into the human spirit to place us in control of ourselves. His Spirit puts our spirit in control so that we are able to function properly. He does all of this, however, only through our willing cooperation. He would never want to make us slaves to his will against our wills.

Scripture makes it clear that sin has no power over us if we are "in" Christ: "We died to sin; how can we live in it any longer?" (Rom. 6:2; see also Rom. 6:7, 18, 22; 8:2). Although we are still able to do wrong things, we are no longer *forced* to do what is wrong as we were when we lived under sin's bondage.

Paul amplified this subject of sin in the flesh in Romans 6:11: "In the same way, count yourselves dead to sin but alive to Christ." Paul is saying that because Christ died and rose again, death no longer has a hold on him; because Christ lives in him, he knows that he has been changed in such a way that sin no longer has power over him. Sin can have a hold on Christians only as long as we believe it can and willingly give in to it. The power of sin has been broken, but we must still change the pattern of sinning. For many of us, sinning has been such a habit that we need Christ's daily help in breaking old patterns.

There is a story of a man who once kept an eagle chained to a stake in the ground. After a period of time the eagle wore a rut in the dirt as he walked around in circles, day after day. One day the eagle was turned loose, but the bird was so accustomed to his circumstance that he just kept walking around in circles inside that old rut.

God wants us to know that we have been freed from sin, and so he is saying, "Realize that you are free and act accordingly. Fly away from sinning." When we are born again we receive power and strength to break habits and patterns of sinning because God gives us his indwelling Holy Spirit.

Some Christians justify living sinfully by saying that the "old nature" is simply too strong and that they are forced to do sinful deeds. But Romans 6:6 says that the old nature, that old self (the old man who is controlled by demon powers) is crucified with Christ. That means it is dead, "rendered powerless, that we should no longer be slaves to sin." When the old man is crucified, the person involved will have no further dealings with the enemy. In fact, 1 John 5:18 says the wicked one does not touch a born-again person. In other words, the enemy cannot compel him to sin. A Christian is dead to his old master. Control can be held over something only as long as that something is alive. When it dies, the powers over it no longer rule. Therefore, since we have taken part in Christ's death, we no longer need to be forced into sin because we have died unto sin with him. However, we can still choose to do sinful things.

The reason Christians commit sinful acts is not found in the compelling power of the old nature but, rather, in the power of unyielded flesh programmed to do wrong through years of consistent habits. Many Christians believe they have two natures—one that does good and the other that does evil. Not so. We either have the "old" nature or the "new" one created by Christ as he enters our lives. Romans 6 clearly tells us that the old nature or man has been crucified and buried. What still exists, however, and what enables us to sin, is our mortal, vulnerable, self-seeking, easily influenced, flesh.

It's no wonder that Christians become confused when they experience some inordinate desire of the flesh and conclude that it is just the old nature acting up. It is impossible for this to happen if indeed one has been crucified with Christ in a salvation experience! The old nature is dead.

Being crucified with Christ is a positional truth. It happens at conversion and is not affected by what we do or do not do. But just what does it mean to be dead to the "old nature" and to be dead to "sin"? In referring to Paul's words in Romans 6:1-2, D. M. Lloyd-Jones suggests, "What [Paul] says about the Christian is that, whereas once he was under the rule and the reign of sin, he is now under the rule and reign of grace. It is either one or the other, he cannot have a foot in each position. He is either under sin or else he is under grace. And I repeat, that what Paul says about us as Christians is that we are dead completely to the rule and reign of sin and evil.[4] But keep in mind that we still live in this present evil age and can be affected by sin.

Once again, Paul's teaching on the co-crucifixion of the believer with Christ is to alert us to the fact that whereas we had no choice but to yield to the power of sin, as the old nature under the power of the enemy forced us to do, now with Christ living within we are not obligated to sin and can therefore choose righteousness.

If it were true that the old nature and the flesh were one and the same, then when the old man died the flesh would die also (Rom. 6:6-7). But nowhere in Scripture does it say that this happens. The flesh is still a very real part of human existence. Nowhere in Scripture are we exhorted to crucify the "old self" again once it is dead. But, rather, many times we are encouraged to keep the flesh in submission (Rom. 6:11; 8:13; 12:1-2; 1 Cor. 9:27; Col. 2:11) and to crucify the evil deeds that want to work through the flesh (Gal. 5:24).

The Christian's responsibility is to live above the flesh, and his new nature will allow him to do this. "Abstain from sinful desires, which war against your soul" (1 Pet. 2:11). "But put on the Lord Jesus Christ, and make no provision for the flesh, to fulfill its lusts" (Rom. 13:14, NKJ). That's the key. Put on the nature of Jesus; become a new creation in Christ!

What substitutions we have had for the New Creation.

We have called it "Forgiveness of Sins," "Being Converted," "Getting Religion," "Joining the Church," and many others.

It is just one thing: A New Creation, a child of God, a partaker of the Divine Nature. These all represent the one fact that you have passed out of death, Satanic Nature, into Life, the realm of God.

That is not just forgiveness of sins, but it is the impartation of a New Nature.

The old self, the old man was crucified with Christ.

A New man was resurrected and when you accepted Jesus Christ as Savior and confessed Him as Lord, God imparted His own Nature, Eternal Life to you and you became "a new species," a new man over which Satan has no dominion.[5]

The true essence of a person, then, is his inner nature, whether "old" or "new." In an unbeliever the old nature will allow the flesh free rein. In a Christian the new inner man, transformed by the Spirit of Christ, helps take control of the flesh and sees to it that it submits to righteousness.

We are able to recognize this new nature as we become aware of an enlightened conscience, the promptings of the Holy Spirit, a desire for righteousness, holiness, and purity, recognition of brothers and sisters in Christ, and a desire to read and know God's Word. It also affirms that Jesus Christ has come in the flesh (1 John 4:2). Keep in mind that before conversion, none of these things were taking place in our lives. Now things are changing radically and drastically because of this new nature.

But what's the real point? It is simply that we can overcome in greater ways if we truly understand the problems we face. If we call the flesh the old nature we may fail to recognize the power of the new nature at the precise time we need it. We may fail to see the body in its rightful place, subject to soul and spirit, and thus allow it liberties it should not have. We may also unconsciously listen to the enemy as he whispers temptations to move the body to sin.

In Corinthians 2:14-15, Paul writes concerning our spiritual, non-spiritual, and worldly selves. (The King James Version of the Bible calls them the spiritual, natural, and carnal). The spiritual man here, of course, belongs to God. But Paul affirms that the man without the Spirit is not a Christian. He is still under demon control. Again, this does not mean that the natural man is not responsible for his sin; God holds every man accountable for his own actions.

Paul also speaks of a worldly (carnal) man, in this case members of the Corinthian church (1 Cor. 3:1). He calls them worldly because they were living in a realm where spiritual life in Christ had taken a backseat to the flesh. They were Christians, but rather than allowing the spirit to reign they were yielding to the dictates of the body in cooperation with the soul.

Satan's demons work hard to energize the flesh. They do this through the minds of those Christians who have not put on the mind of Christ (1 Cor. 2:16). These Christians are saved—Christ has come to live in their hearts—but their wills are still in the process of being surrendered to all that is righteous in him. Thus the will cooperates with the senses of the body and allows these senses to be turned loose.

We need to fill our minds with "whatever is true, whatever is noble, whatever is right, whatever is pure, whatever is lovely, whatever is admirable" (Phil. 4:8) on a day-to-day basis. In that way we "will be able to test and approve what God's will is—his good, pleasing and perfect will" (Rom. 12:1).

Sinful men looked at the early church and said, "These people are turning the world upside down" (see Acts 17:6). If you are standing on your head, then right-side-up will look upside down. The truth is that God, through those early disciples, was turning the world right-side-up. God was bringing uprightness into focus. He was making it possible for sin to no longer rule over mortal bodies. The body could once again take its proper place and become subject to the soul and spirit. Keep in mind that the body, by itself, is not sinful or evil; but when the body is out of order in relationship to soul and spirit it misses the mark and becomes a channel for sin. The body in its rightful position is good. Every part has a function in God's plan and none of those parts should be looked upon with contempt or disrespect.

Frequently, Satan is blamed for our sinning. "The devil made me do it" often is the excuse when we succumb to the force of sin—a force more powerful than personal resistance outside of Christ. Certainly, satanic influence plays havoc with the flesh and at times causes sin. But if sin is to be overcome, we must not always blame Satan. Our problems are due to separation from God and the resulting inability to deal with life, as well as to Satan and his demons. Each must be properly identified and dealt with according to God's Word. We must deal with the power of sin caused by that separation and not blame Satan for its consequences. The gospel of Jesus Christ is God's way of dealing with sin. "Christ in you" becomes the solution to sin in you.

So, we have the world and the flesh to contend with; but we also have the devil and his influence.

OVERCOMING THE DEVIL

In chapter 1 we covered a good deal of information concerning Satan. Now we need to see that we have been given power and authority over him. It is important that we realize how strong the world and the flesh are as they fight against us. But one of our toughest battles is against the "spiritual forces of evil" (Eph. 6:12). We need to fight on all three battlefronts throughout our Christian lives.

Gigi Graham Tchividjian, daughter of Billy Graham, tells of an incident from her childhood. The children in the family were singing "I've Got the Joy, Joy, Joy, Joy Down in My Heart." When they reached the last verse, "And if the devil doesn't like it, he can sit on a tack . . . ," her father said, "I don't want you to sing that verse anymore. The devil does a very good job of being a devil, and I think it is wrong to take him lightly or mock him. He is real and powerful, and he is no joking matter."[6]

Even though the word *devil* doesn't appear in the Old Testament, he has always been around to harass God's people. He is called by such other names as Satan, the serpent, Lucifer, and the adversary. We first encounter the term *devil* in Matthew 4:1, where Jesus was led by the Spirit into the desert to be tempted by the devil. Jesus had just been baptized in the Jordan River by John the Baptist. Then the Spirit of God descended on him and God spoke from heaven, "This is my Son, whom I love; with him I am well pleased" (Matt. 3:16-17). And, just as he does with us when we receive the Holy Spirit upon being born again—or when we are doing anything that is pleasing to God—the devil, "the tempter," came to Jesus and began to hound him.

Christ came to earth to destroy the devil's work (1 John 3:8). His mission was to destroy Satan's kingdom and deliver mankind from his power. However, this act of love and mercy toward humanity was not to be done unilaterally. God does not say, "It doesn't matter what mankind wants." Rather, he invites us to give expression to our own personal free will and become actively involved in the war at hand. We find a purpose and a reason for being when we enter the fight against Satan and rebellion.

Because of Christ we are once again on the verge of ruling our own lives under his universal plan. Because of the indwelling Spirit of Christ, we have power far greater than that of the demon spirits. Redeemed man is now a threat to Satan's kingdom. Jesus said, "I have given you authority to trample on snakes and scorpions, and to overcome all the power of the enemy; nothing will harm you. However, do not rejoice that the spirits submit to you, but rejoice that your names are written in heaven" (Luke 10:19-20).

Jesus, speaking to Peter, said, "I will build my church and the gates of hell shall not prevail against it" (Matt. 16:18, KJV). All of his followers who believed on him were about to learn of the power of the Messiah against the enemy, a power that would literally cause evil spiritual forces to have need of fortification. Notice the words "gates of hell." Gates imply a fortress built for defense. Whereas Satan, as the ruler of this world, feared little before Calvary, now he has to contend with Christ's powerful army of Spirit-filled believers. This forces Satan's army to take refuge. And Jesus guaranteed that no gate erected by the enemy would stand. A mighty host—his Church, his followers—would conquer all resistance.

Such power encompasses the use of heaven's power of attorney. "I will give you the keys of the kingdom of heaven; whatever you bind on earth will be bound in heaven, and whatever you loose on earth will be loosed in heaven" (Matt. 16:19). Keys imply authority. For the first time since Adam, man would have power against demons and disease: "he gave them power and authority to drive out all demons and to cure diseases" (Luke 9:1); "Lord, even the demons submit to us in your name" (10:17); "Is any one of you sick? . . . pray over him and anoint him with oil in the name of the Lord. And the prayer offered in faith will make the sick person well" (James 5:14). And whether we want to believe it or not, all of this power and authority is available to believers in the twentieth century. It worked two thousand years ago and it still works today. It works because Jesus Christ is still the same today.

"Awesome," you may say as you look at the dynamic power for coming against Satan's kingdom. But when

Christ says, "I tell you the truth, anyone who has faith in me will do what I have been doing. He will do even greater things than these because I am going to the Father" (John 14:12), the potential for fighting Satan goes far beyond what the human mind can comprehend. However, this power to overcome sin and Satan is available only through Jesus Christ. It is not some magical force called down and exercised at will. It is the outcome of a close relationship with God. It is the exercise of invested authority.

Some in the Church today seem to be hung up on power, struggling for places of preeminence. They want to work mighty works at their own bidding. They forget, or ignore, the truth that without Christ we can do nothing (John 15:5). Without his directing, inspiring, and guiding we cannot operate effectively or with authority. Yet numbers of Christians have a "ye are gods" mentality that causes them to try to attack Satan's domain without the Captain of our salvation leading in the fight.

Satan is a defeated foe. He was conquered at Calvary. Soon we shall see the sentence carried out and rejoice that we were given the opportunity to be a part of putting down the rebellion. "That's right," you say, "that's what I read in my Bible. But where is all this power and authority? Where is the victory? Why does it appear that I am losing much of the time? Why don't I see the mighty answers to prayer that God guarantees in his word?" These are honest questions asked by Christians who feel defeated, or by those who genuinely weigh what they see in this life against what they read in Scripture.

But if you look carefully you will see that the Church is not suffering defeat. There are tremendous victories being won worldwide. Christ's army is moving forward. Great numbers of people are being saved, lives are being changed, relationships restored, and multitudes of personal prayers are being answered, giving testimony to God's powerful army on the move.

Those of us who have not seen the victories we would like to see need to develop the attitude that we are going to seek God until we find why we are powerless. And most often we will find that powerlessness comes from prayerlessness.

I once heard the story of a church that decided to believe God for healing. Members began to pray but with no apparent results. Months passed and still no answers, yet they continued to pray for the sick. Eventually these folks began to see miracles; today they see many. In this case, prayer and persistence eventually brought victory.

In the next chapter we will look at ways we can defend ourselves against the enemy.

NOTES

1. Dick Eastman, *The University of the Word* (Ventura, Calif.: Regal Books, 1983), 106.
2. *Humanist Manifestos I and II* (Buffalo, N.Y.: Prometheus Books, 1977), 16-19.
3. The will of man is the major concern as to whether we focus on "things above" creating "spiritual man" or on "things below" creating "fleshly man." The word "body" here does not refer to natural flesh, the inanimate object it would be without soul and spirit. It refers to the choices and dispositions within us that are oriented to serve sin though the body. It is important to understand that as we continue to make choices to sin we eventually lose our ability to carry out the subsequent choices we would like to make; sin becomes increasingly powerful as it uses the body for its purposes. The body is the instrument, not the instigator (although it almost appears otherwise because so much power is resident in its senses). Furthermore, I have no desire to promote gnosticism which says that "spirit is good" and "matter is evil." God created the physical universe (including our bodies) as good. It is using good things incorrectly that constitutes perversion.
4. D. M. Lloyd-Jones, *Romans: The New Man (6)* (Grand Rapids: Zondervan, 1972), 21.
5. E. W. Kenyon, *In His Presence* (Seattle, Wash.: Kenyon's Gospel Publishing Society, 1944), 38.
6. Gigi Graham Tchividjian, *Sincerely* (Grand Rapids: Zondervan, 1984), 20.

SIX

Arming for Defense

In the previous chapter we described the enemies we face. In this chapter we are going to look more closely at the power that is available to help us overcome Satan and his forces. Then we will look at the defensive weapons we need in order to keep from being overcome.

When we talk about power we mean the same power Jesus had, the same authority; the same power he used in the wilderness to fight temptation and the power he employed to work miracles. Yes, tremendous power is available to the believer. Power against sin, against Satan, against sickness and disease, and against the world system. Not magical power; not power as an impersonal energy source; and not power void of God. But power from the source of all power and authority both in heaven and in earth—*power by relationship*. Scripture declares, "The people who *know* their God shall be strong, and carry out great exploits" (Dan. 11:32, NKJV, italics added). And this power exists because God's conditions have been met. But it can only work in us if we are prepared.

PREPARATIONS FOR POWER

The victory that comes as a result of the manifestation of God's power, as well as any other blessing from him, is conditional. There are certain steps we must follow in order for him to fulfill his promises. These steps are usually very simple for anyone who is sincere about his or her relationship with God. Let's take a brief look at some of the steps that are basic to defense in spiritual warfare.

Knowledge of God's Word. In warfare, ignorance of the enemy can cause defeat. How can any army operate effectively if it doesn't know the tactics of those it is fighting? The Apostle Paul fought Satan well and offered this affirmation as part of the reason for his success: "For we are not unaware of his [Satan's] schemes" (2 Cor 2:11). Evidently Paul never took Satan for granted. He no doubt studied, searched, and pursued ways to understand the demonic realm. He didn't become preoccupied with it, but he certainly became aware of it to avoid being deceived. Charles Swindoll cautions: "Before any opponent can be intelligently withstood, a knowledge of his ways must be known. Ignorance must be dispelled. No boxer in his right mind enters the ring without having first studied the other boxer's style. The same is true on the football field. Or the battlefield. Days (sometimes *months)* are spent studying the tactics, the weaknesses, the strengths of the opponent. Ignorance is an enemy to victory."[1]

In the Old Testament God says, "My people are destroyed from lack of knowledge" (Hos. 4:6). Many have the idea that just "being a Christian" is good enough. "Since you belong to God, sit back and relax. He will take care of you. After all, God will put a hedge around you so that Satan can't get through. Forget Satan. He'll go away. Just don't talk about him." And though it is a tragic truth that some dwell too much on themes related to Satan and demons, the enemy himself would like believers to ignore his existence. Is it any wonder that some Christians are sometimes overwhelmed by him?

Resisting the Sins of the Flesh. As we discussed in chapter 1, sin causes separation from God and that separation allows Satan to gain control. Sinning becomes a hindrance to the power needed to combat the Evil One especially when it is a known sin. "Anyone, then, who knows the good he ought to do and doesn't do it, sins" (James 4:17). We read a description of the sins of the flesh in Galatians 5:19-21. God's Word is careful to record them so that we are aware of what will keep power out of our lives.

Keep in mind that all people have trouble with sinning, even though the power of sin has been taken care of in a Christian's life. That is why God, in 1 John 1:9, provides a solution to the problem. But a Christian is not to live a life of committing sinful deeds. He is not to think that the grace of God allows him, once he is saved, to go on living any way he pleases (Rom. 6:1-2). When Jesus confronted the adultress he told her to "go now and leave your life of sin" (John 8:11). The writer of Hebrews told his readers to "throw off . . . the sin that so easily entangles" (Heb. 12:1). Paul told the Corinthians, "Flee from sexual immorality" (1 Cor. 6:18) and "flee from idolatry" (10:14). He told Timothy to "flee the evil desires of youth, and pursue righteousness, faith, love and peace" (2 Tim. 2:22). In this admonition we see that it is not enough just to forsake sin. We must put something else in its place: righteousness, faith, love, and peace.

Relinquish the Cares of this Life. Because this planet is in rebellion and because there is a war going on, it is essential to give undivided attention to the Captain of our salvation. As most soldiers know, there are times when many of the good and legitimate pleasures of this life have to be put aside to ensure victory. This does not mean God's people must live ascetic lives, that they cannot enjoy life or experience pleasure. It simply means that sacrifices must be made to win the war.

When a nation is faced with sending its men off to battle, that nation brings certain demands upon its soldiers in order to save lives and protect national interest. The same is true in spiritual warfare. Strict demands must be made on all soldiers of the Cross in order to triumph. Ralph Winter suggests that "we must be willing to adopt a wartime life-style if we are to play fair with the clear intent of Scripture that the poor of this earth, the people who sit in darkness, shall see a great light."

Materialism, riches, and even the necessities of life can cause distraction. Scripture warns against misplaced priorities. Jesus said, "Seek first [God's] kingdom and his righteousness" (Matt. 6:33). It is easy to preach a materialistic gospel that makes God look like a divine errand boy or a big sugar daddy in the sky. There is nothing wrong with preaching that God will meet all our needs—if we meet his conditions. However, some preach that there ought to be a fine car in every driveway, along with any number of other luxuries. And soon our focus is not on the warfare but on materialism.

Again, there is nothing wrong with having good things in this life. But material possessions become wrong when they occupy our center of attention. The same is true even with the basic necessities needed for living. If Jesus were to expound on Matthew 6:25-34, we might find him saying, "As important as food and clothing are, you must realize that the battle being waged in the heavenlies needs to be your first priority.

Don't worry or be concerned about secondary matters. If your Father can take care of birds and flowers, which he does quite easily, then it will be an easy matter for him to take care of your needs as well."

How often we are tempted with one of Satan's subtle deceptions. "Just take enough time to get ahead monetarily. Once you have reached financial security, you will be able to serve God better. You won't have to worry about money." What a lie! And sadly, many Christians fall for it. Many spend a major portion of their time and lives seeking riches rather than God— riches that can never secure happiness or a place in God's kingdom. If we place our confidence and security in money, what shall we do with God's promises and provisions (Matthew 6), or with his promise to supply all of our needs (Phil. 4:19)?

True, we need to pursue life's needs and fulfill basic obligations, but only after first seeking the kingdom. "People who want to get rich fall into temptation and a trap, and into many foolish and harmful desires that plunge men into ruin and destruction" (1 Tim. 6:9). It isn't the riches that give people trouble, it's the *desire* for them and the constant attention people place on them. Scripture doesn't say, "Where your heart is, there will your treasure be also." It says, "Where your treasure is, there will your heart be also" (Matt. 6:21, KJV). If we treasure the things of God, our hearts will be his.

Conquering Spiritual Pride. Most who have ever been used effectively by the Lord will, no doubt, confirm that pride is no small enemy. According to Paul Billheimer:

> Very few can take honors, either from the world or from God, without becoming conceited. What servant of the Lord does not know the subtle temptation to

spiritual pride that follows even mediocre success? How often one relates an answer to prayer in such a way as to reflect credit upon oneself—and then ends up blandly saying "To God be the glory." The ego is so swollen by the fall that it is an easy prey for Satan and his demons. . . .

Who knows how much God would do for his servants if he dared. If one does not boast openly following an anointed fluency of speech, a specific answer to prayer, a miracle of faith or some other manifestation of spiritual gifts, or even graces, he is tempted to gloat secretly because of the recognition. Except for special grace on such occasions, one falls easily into Satan's trap. Because most men are so vulnerable to any small stimulus to pride, God, although he loves to do so, dares not honor many before the world by special displays of his miracle-working power in answer to prayer.[2]

It is absolutely necessary for God to deal with pride before we can be used in any meaningful way. Billheimer continues:

> For until God has wrought a work of true humility and brokenness in his servants, he cannot answer some of their prayers without undue risk of producing the pride that goes before a fall. If God could trust the petitioner to keep lowly, who knows how many more answers to prayer he could readily give?[3]

Power, mighty power, is available to the believer who prepares properly to receive it. However, God has special timing for much of what he does. Unfortunately, it is often difficult to understand this concept, and discouragement can set in easily when things don't happen as fast as anticipated.

Although we have tremendous power available to us,

we still need God's armor to shield us from attack. And God's Word speaks in specific terms concerning this armor.

WEAPONS FOR DEFENSE

"The weapons we fight with are not the weapons of the world. On the contrary, they have divine power to demolish strongholds" (2 Cor. 10:4). This divine power becomes available to us only when we yield properly to the Holy Spirit. Such power makes both offensive and defensive weapons operative and effective. The following is what God's Word describes as weapons for defense—the Christian soldier's armor that will protect us in battle: "Be strong in the Lord and in his mighty power. Put on the full armor of God so that you can take your stand against the devil's schemes. For our struggle is not against flesh and blood, but against the rulers, against the authorities, against the powers of this dark world and against the spiritual forces of evil in the heavenly realms" (Eph. 6:10-12).

The Greek word translated "schemes" in this passage is *methodeias*, from which we get our English word methods. *Methodeias* are the cunning devices and plans Satan uses to enslave, deceive, and ruin the souls of men. Many who realize the reality of this warfare are tempted to become fearful, but instead of a run-and-hide-the-devil's-after-me attitude we are to be powerful soldiers who rise to the cause and stop Satan through prayer and the Word of God. Then we are to pursue him as he turns to run. We must learn to take an offensive stand. This is God's plan for dealing with the enemy. Then and only then will there be fewer casualties and greater victories.

"Therefore put on the full armor of God, so that when the day of evil comes, you may be able to stand your ground, and after you have done everything, to stand. Stand firm then, with the belt of truth buckled around your waist, with the breastplate of righteousness in place, and with your feet fitted with the readiness that comes from the gospel of peace. In addition to all this, take up the shield of faith, with which you can extinguish all the flaming arrows of the evil one. Take the helmet of salvation and the sword of the Spirit, which is the word of God. And pray in the Spirit on all occasions with all kinds of prayers and requests" (Eph. 6:13-18).

The Belt of Truth. In the time of the early church, Roman soldiers used large belts or girdles to cover their lower stomachs, reproductive organs, and upper thighs. These leather straps not only protected them but also were used to carry some of the weapons used in warfare such as knives and daggers. Likewise, the Christian's belt of truth represents protection of the teachings of the gospel as opposed to the deceptive teachings of the enemy and the world.

Satan has spread his false teachings and established myriad cults throughout human existence. From the insidious idea that truth is relative—that it is different things to different people—to the claim that Jesus is no different than any other man, we are bombarded with lies from the evil one. We must be protected by the truth of the gospel. Jesus said, "If you hold to my teaching, you are really my disciples. Then you will know the truth, and the truth will set you free" (John 8:31-32). Just as the Roman soldier had freedom of movement with his weapons mounted on his belt, we have freedom because we are girded in the truth of Jesus Christ.

A popular, cynical, pessimistic question that has come down through the ages seems to be the philosophical inquiry, "What is truth?" This is what Pilate asked after Jesus told him that he "came into the world, to testify to the truth" (John 18:37-38). Of course, Pilate didn't really want to know the truth. To know the truth calls for action on our part. It means that we must make decisions concerning righteousness and evil.

Jesus said, "I am the way and the truth and the life" (John 14:6). He could have said, "When you know me you will know truth." Edmon C. Gruss explains, "The Bible-believing Christian cannot accept the popular statement that 'all religions lead to the same place.' Instead, he accepts the Bible's promise that one *can know the truth,* for ultimate TRUTH is not a system—an 'it'—but a *Person,* Jesus Christ ('I am . . . the truth,' John 14:6). Truth to the Christian is also conformity to the revealed will of God as set forth in the Bible."[4]

Truth begins in the spiritual realm and proceeds to the natural. It begins with Jesus and ends with conformity to the blueprint of creation. In one sphere it's a person, and in the other sphere it's the manifestation of that person in righteous actions and deeds. This is why Christ's Spirit must live inside a person in order for him or her to be righteous. There are many who want to clean up their lives to be righteous so that God will accept them. It won't work. Righteousness is not possible outside of Christ.

It is easier to understand truth as a person by recognizing the power a creator has over what he fashions. A painter becomes the truth to what he is painting when he places the borders, determines the colors, and chooses the setting. His personality is expressed in his work, and his work is a reflection of who he is. He has the right to paint each segment in the picture as he desires. It is his painting.

Christ is the truth in creation because he created the

physical and spiritual universe. "He is the image of the invisible God, the firstborn over all creation. For *by him all things were created:* things in heaven and on earth, visible and invisible, whether thrones or powers or rulers or authorities; *all things were created by him* and for him. He is before all things, and in him all things hold together" (Col. 1:15-17, italics added). "In the beginning was the Word, and the Word was with God, and the Word was God. He was with God in the beginning. *Through him all things were made;* without him nothing was made that has been made" (John 1:1-3, italics added). "In times past God spoke to our forefathers through the prophets at many times and in various ways, but in these last days he has spoken to us by his Son, whom he appointed heir of all things, and *through whom he made the universe*" (Heb. 1:1-2, italics added).

Of course, truth has a counterpart—falsehood. And rebellion is falsehood at work. The purpose of the insurrection was to replace God with Satan. In seeking to be like God, Satan takes truth and twists it into falsehood. He is the great deceiver. As Jesus is the embodiment of truth, so the enemy is the embodiment of falsehood. "He [the devil] was a murderer from the beginning, not holding to the truth, for there is no truth in him. When he lies, he speaks his native language, for he is a liar and the father of lies" (John 8:44). Those who follow the enemy are involved in the same thing. Romans 1:25 says that they have "exchanged the truth of God for a lie." A denial of truth and an open embrace of falsehood can, and often does, lead to demon possession. The enemy finds great delight in and gains much control over one who denies truth.

Where then is truth to be found? In Jesus Christ! And where is Jesus Christ to be found? In the Word of

God! It is out of this book that the truth of God will flow into any heart opened to him.

The Breastplate of Righteousness. After the belt of truth, Paul then exhorts the Ephesians, and us, to put in place the breastplate of righteousness. The breastplate, of course, protects the soldier's heart, the organ that pumps life throughout the entire body.

In speaking of the heart we are referring basically to that which is spirit. Righteousness, then, protects the human spirit. It keeps the spirit from being overcome by elements of the soul, the senses of the body, and evil spirits.

How is righteousness determined? How does one become righteous? First, we cannot get it on our own; it comes only through faith in Jesus Christ. In 1 Corinthians 5:21 it says, "God made him [Christ] who had no sin to be sin for us, so that in him we might become the righteousness of God." When you accept Jesus as your Savior and become a new creation you "put off your old self, which is being corrupted by its deceitful desires" and are "made new in the attitude of your minds," putting "on the new self, created to be like God in true righteousness and holiness" (Eph. 4:22-24).

Our own good deeds are worthless if we have not taken on the righteousness of Christ. God sees us as justified only on the basis of the righteousness of Christ. Good works are the outworking, or result, of Christ living in us.

Satan has led some in the world into believing that a "righteous" person is a simpleminded, uneducated, biased person who sits around all day reading the Bible and spends half the night praying. God, of course, is pictured as a cruel, harsh, malevolent tyrant who is concerned only about eternity and cares little for the present and who has a way of shouting, "Thou shalt have no fun." Hayford in his book *Prayer is Invading the Impossible* further adds:

> The image of a frowning God, brooding in anger and perched on the edge of a ten-mile-high cliff with a quiver of lightning bolts ready for hurling at the unsuspecting and the helpless, must be smashed.[5]

What is so incredible is that with all the love God has given to the human race, we still fall for these distortions from Satan. We somehow fail to see that God is offering us abundant life *now*—inner joy, happiness, security, and peace.

When we perform right actions and deeds, Satan's plans are countered and our own spirits protected. When we live in such a way that our vertical and horizontal relationships are in order, we are able to have a clear conscience before both God and man (Acts 24:16). And Satan finds it difficult to attack us because he has no legitimate means for doing so. He must then resort to false accusations.

"For you were once darkness, but now you are light in the Lord. Live as children of light (for the fruit of the light consists in all goodness, righteousness and truth) and find out what pleases the Lord. Have nothing to do with the fruitless deeds of darkness, but rather expose them" (Eph. 5:7).

Feet Fitted with Readiness. The next piece of armor is good footwear. Paul spoke of having "feet fitted with the readiness that comes from the gospel of peace." Isaiah said, "How beautiful on the mountains are the feet of those who bring good news, who proclaim peace, who bring good tidings, who proclaim salvation, who say to Zion, 'Your God reigns!' " (52:7). This verse, which the Apostle Paul quoted in Romans 10:15, could also have been the verse he was thinking of when he spoke of this piece of armor.

The word *peace* is strongly associated with our Lord and Savior. At his birth the angels heralded his coming saying, "Peace to men on whom his favor rests" (Luke 2:14). Jesus told his disciples to "be at peace with each other" (Mark 9:50); then just before his violent death he said to his followers, "Peace I leave with you; my peace I give you. . . . Do not let your hearts be troubled and do not be afraid" (John 14:27). Truly, we Christians have the good news of peace.

But it isn't ours to keep to ourselves. We are to put on our "fitted" shoes and go out into battle. To be fitted means to be individually prepared. And the Bible spells out very clearly how we do this.

First, we must stay up-to-date with God. This covers at least three areas:

1. Bible study. Later Paul tells us to take the "sword of the Spirit, which is the word of God." Oh that believers would see how essential it is to live deeply within God's Word. Remember, Jesus fought Satan in the wilderness with the Word of God.

2. Prayer. "Pray continually," Paul said to the people in Thessalonica (1 Thess. 5:17). This doesn't mean we have to go around with our eyes closed and our hands folded all the time; it does mean we constantly should be aware of God's presence and power within us and include him in our conversation and our every action. It also means that we need a regular quiet time with him.

3. Fellowship with other believers. "Let us not give up meeting together," the author of Hebrews said, "but let us encourage one another—and all the more as you see the Day approaching" (10:25). It is in meeting together, sharing together, upholding one another, weeping, laughing, planning our strategy together that we

are able to overcome. We cannot stand against Satan effectively by ourselves. We need one another.

Second, we must be ready to do good. There are at least two elements to this:

1. Be generous with finances. Jesus, in his Sermon on the Mount, told his disciples to "give, and it will be given to you. A good measure, pressed down, shaken together and running over, will be poured into your lap. For with the measure you use, it will be measured to you" (Luke 6:38). He isn't talking only about tithing in this verse; he means we are to give generously to others who are obviously in need. Concerning tithes the Lord said, "Bring the whole tithe into the storehouse, that there may be food in my house. Test me in this . . . and see if I will not throw open the floodgates of heaven and pour out so much blessing that you will not have room enough for it" (Mal. 3:10).

2. Be unselfish with time. Jesus told the parable about the Good Samaritan who took time to help a man who had been stripped of his clothes, beaten, and left half dead by a band of thieves. He took the time to help someone in need. We live in a rush-rush world. We never seem to have time for people. It takes nurturing on a one-to-one basis to lead another person to Jesus. Fit your feet with the gospel of peace—a gospel that has time for others.

The Shield of Faith. "Take up the shield of faith, with which you can extinguish all the flaming arrows of the evil one" (Eph. 6:16). The soldiers in Paul's day used shields to protect them in hand-to-hand combat, but the shields also sheltered them from the enemy's burning arrows. The "flaming arrows" the evil one shoots at the Christian soldier are not just the day-by-day problems, trials, tests, and temptations that come to all of us. We cannot escape these situations even with the shield of faith because, as Peter says, we should rejoice if "now for a little while you may have had to suffer grief in all kinds of trials. These have come so that your faith—of greater worth than gold, which perishes even though refined by fire—may be proved genuine and may result in praise, glory and honor when Jesus Christ is revealed" (1 Pet. 1:6-7).

If the shield of faith protected us from all trials, the strongest and most faithful of us would never have difficult experiences in our Christian walk. But in Paul's list of his own sufferings (2 Cor. 11:24-27) we see that the active soldier is a soldier under attack.

In the great contest for Job's loyalty, God allowed Satan to nearly destroy this man. One after another, his possessions were snatched away. Five hundred yoke of oxen, five hundred donkeys, seven thousand sheep, three thousand camels, and most of his "large number" of servants and herdsmen were killed or carried off by enemy raiders. Then his ten children all died at once when a house they were in collapsed. As if that weren't enough, the devil then attacked Job's body with painful sores. But through all of this, even though Job couldn't understand why all these things were happening, he maintained his faithfulness to God.

No, the shield of faith is not to protect us from the experience of trials. But it *does* protect us from the by-products of trials—fear, hopelessness, despair, murmuring, complaining, and temptation. Paul could say, "We are hard pressed on every side, but not crushed; perplexed, but not in despair; persecuted, but not abandoned; struck down, but not destroyed" (2 Cor. 4:8-9). And Job, in the midst of his grief and physical suffering, as he scraped his sores with pieces of broken pottery while he sat in ashes, exclaimed, "As long as I have . . . the breath of God in my nostrils . . . I will maintain my righteousness and never let it go" (Job 27:3,6). Both Paul and Job carried the shield of faith.

What is the shield of faith? Where is it found? How is it taken up?

The best-known faith verse in the Bible is in Hebrews. "Faith is being sure of what we hope for and certain of what we do not see" (Heb. 11:1). The writer of Hebrews recounts the names of those people of the Old Testament who lived by faith. These people trusted in God's justice, love, and sovereignty regardless of the trials they went through. They carried their shield of faith. Faith is believing God when there is no outward encouragement, when the evidence of hope cannot be seen. The verb form of *faith* in the Greek is translated "believe" in the New Testament; believe in God, believe God.

How do we get faith? Consider these four ways: (1) by hearing and reading the Word of God; (2) by acting on the faith we already have; (3) by seeking Jesus; and (4) by living in Christ. Let's take a closer look at these elements.

First of all, faith begins with God. There is no untapped reservoir of faith residing in the human frame. All faith comes from God. And God puts this faith in us by the hearing of his Word: "Faith comes from hearing the message, and the message is heard through the word of Christ" (Rom. 10:17). Dwight L. Moody, the great evangelist of the nineteenth century, declared, "I prayed for faith and thought that some day faith would come down and strike me like lightning. But faith did not seem to come. One day I read in the tenth chapter of Romans, 'Faith cometh by hearing, and hearing by the Word of God.' I had (up to this time) closed my Bible and prayed for faith. I now opened my Bible and began to study, and faith has been growing ever since."

Second, after we have our initial faith we increase it by acting upon it: "Make every effort to add to your faith goodness; and to goodness, knowledge; and to

knowledge, self-control; and to self-control, perseverance; and to perseverance, godliness; and to godliness,
brotherly kindness; and to brotherly kindness, love.
For if you possess these qualities in increasing measure, they will keep you from being ineffective and
unproductive in your knowledge of our Lord Jesus
Christ" (2 Pet. 1:5-8). By putting today's faith to work,
we receive greater portions of faith for tomorrow.
Faith, when it is neglected, dies. When it is used it
grows. Thus, we go from faith to faith (Rom. 1:17).

In the story *The Robe,* Demetrius, the Greek slave,
tries to explain his faith in Jesus to his master, Marcel-
lus, "This faith . . . is not like a deed to a house in
which one may live with full rights of possession. It is
more like a kit of tools with which a man may build
him a house. The tools will be worth just what he does
with them. When he lays them down, they will have no
value until he takes them up again."[6]

Third, we get greater faith by seeking Jesus. The
author of Hebrews, after listing the great men of faith
in the Old Testament, concluded by saying, "Therefore,
since we are surrounded by such a great cloud of witnesses, let us throw off everything that hinders and
the sin that so easily entangles, and let us run with
perseverance the race marked out for us. Let us fix our
eyes on Jesus, the *author and perfecter of our faith,*
who for the joy set before him endured the cross,
scorning its shame, and sat down at the right hand of
the throne of God" (Heb. 12:1-2, italics added).

During the 1984 Olympic games held in California,
Joan Benoit of the U.S. took an early lead in the wom-
en's marathon and maintained that lead to win the
gold medal after 26.2 miles. It was an exciting event.
But even more dramatic was the finish of Gabriela
Andersen-Schiess of Switzerland, who staggered into
the Coliseum suffering from heat prostration. She
waved off those who would come to her aid—she

wanted no interference to her finishing the race. She finished thirty-seventh out of the forty-four who completed the marathon. She said she thought the finish was "right there," at the end of the Olympic Coliseum tunnel. She didn't know she still had to run more than four hundred meters. But she kept on, one painful step at a time, enduring her pain, until she finished the course. She saw the "joy set before" her. How much more joy is in store for those of us who are seeking "the prize for which God has called me heavenward in Christ Jesus" (Phil. 3:14).

The Apostle Paul told Timothy, his "true son in the faith," that he had "fought the good fight" and "finished the race, I have kept the faith" (2 Tim. 4:7).

Finally, faith becomes stronger as we live (abide, remain) in Christ. When faith is operating in a Christian he has nothing in or of himself to glory about; for it is really the faith of Christ that is working in him— faith he received as a gift from God (Eph. 2:8). "I have been crucified with Christ and I no longer live, but Christ lives in me. The life I live in the body, I live by *faith in the Son of God,* who loved me and gave himself for me" (Gal. 2:2). Jesus said much about placing our faith in Him. John 15 illustrates this close living by describing Jesus as the true vine and us as the branches. Furthermore Jesus says that "if a man remains in me and I in him, he will bear much fruit; apart from me you can do nothing" (v. 5). We increase our faith by remaining in him.

Faith is not the door to abundance. Faith is the door to God. Currently there is preaching that suggests that faith is the way to fulfill all materialistic and spiritual desires—and the heaviest emphasis is placed upon the material. Certainly faith is needed in order to receive anything from God. That cannot be denied. But frequently the desire is to use this unique power for self-serving purposes. Faith then becomes a kind of plaything.

Misinstructed, we may try to find faith similarly within ourselves as we are instructed in some non-Christian teachings to look within ourselves until God is found. We then become faith seekers rather than God seekers. Faith, in many ways, becomes a substitute for God himself. When men advocate having faith in faith, there is danger of missing the biblical directive which says, "Have faith in God" (Mark 11:22).

But what is faith? Since it operates within the spirit it becomes difficult to fully describe. Probably the simplest way to explain it would be to say that it is the supernatural touch of the Holy Spirit on the human spirit creating an awareness of truth.

The woman who came to Jesus and touched his garment was healed when she sought the Healer. She probably did not sit down to try to measure her faith, nor is it likely that she had ever read anything on faith. She perhaps knew little if anything about the subject. This woman had a need and, rather than complaining about it, she set out to get her problem solved. Her need was met when she came in contact with the Lord.

The problem with many people who want faith and don't have much is that the different parts of their three-fold being are still in disarray. Their bodies and souls still control their spirits. This forces their spirits into submission and keeps faith ineffective. Then, try as they may to conjure it up in their minds, they wind up with nothing more than a spiritual headache. The spirit must be in control for faith to be operative.

Doubt is often thought of as being the opposite of faith. Whereas doubt is certainly a hindrance to faith (see Matt. 21:21), unbelief is in greater opposition. If doubt can slow down or even temporarily stop faith, unbelief can completely destroy it. Unbelief is a heavy element of rebellion. It is, basically, refusing to seek the truth. Most of us doubt at one time or another. Yet, by continuing to seek truth in Jesus Christ, doubt dissipates. But doubt will not diffuse if the heart is closed to truth. Eventually that doubt will turn to unbelief, and that will cause spiritual bankruptcy.

Abraham and Sarah doubted God's promise concerning their yet-to-be-conceived son, Isaac. This could be expected because of their ages. But notice Abraham "did not waver through *unbelief* regarding the promise of God, but was strengthened in his faith and gave glory to God" (Rom. 4:20, italics added). In spite of doubt, Abraham continued seeking God, refusing unbelief. In doing so, his doubt was eventually conquered.

The disciples once tried to cast an evil spirit out of an epileptic and failed. After Jesus cast the spirit out, the disciples were troubled. Had not Christ given them "power and authority over all the power of the enemy?" Then what went wrong? Why, suddenly, did the power cease to flow? Christ's answer was blunt: "Because of your unbelief" (Matt. 17:20, KJV). Andrew Murray says, "The power the disciples had received to cast out devils did not belong to them as a permanent gift or possession. The power was in Christ, to be received, held, and used by faith alone, living faith in Himself."[7]

But, why this unbelief? Things had been going well, then all of a sudden it was as if the fire had run out of fuel. And that is exactly what had happened. The disciples had failed to "make contact" on a continual basis with the "author and finisher of our faith" (Heb. 12:2). They had run dry. They needed to make contact once again with the spiritual dimension in Christ Jesus.

Once the spirit becomes Christ-centered and faith is in operation, we are able to control our minds. "We take captive every thought to make it obedient to Christ" (2 Cor. 10:5). The fiery darts of the enemy, those evil thoughts, accusations, and fears cannot enter into the spirit through the mind; thus they fall harmlessly, as do arrows that glance feebly off a shield. It is certainly true that the mind will continue to be the target of Satan's arrows. But when they strike, our "wills," when operating correctly, allow us to "take captive" the present evil suggestion and "make it obedient to Christ."

By no means does the mind become passive when it is submitted to Christ. In fact, it becomes far more active in the realm of good, constructive, and creative thought. It is simply that when it is controlled by the spirit the mind isn't obligated or forced into evil thinking.

The Helmet of Salvation. When Jesus Christ enters a life, *immediately that person's spirit is saved.* There is a passing from death to life. No longer is he subject to eternal damnation, but, rather, he is guaranteed a glorious place with God throughout eternity. The soul, however, is slow in coming to full submission to Christlikeness. We can say then, that a person's soul, which includes his mind, is being saved (Phil. 2:15). In this process we are encouraged to let the mind of Christ be in us. As we walk with him, our minds are changed and renewed continuously, always bringing us closer to his image (2 Cor. 3:18).

The body, however, is yet to be saved. And it will not be saved until mortality puts on immortality when the body is resurrected. While here on earth, in its corruptible state, the body is subject to sickness, disease, and injury. It grows old and dies. It is far from the state that God intends it to be. Thus, the spirit is saved; the soul is being saved; and the body will be saved; but, none of this will happen outside of a personal relationship with the Man-God, Jesus Christ. God's Word says, "For there is no other name under heaven given to men by which we must be saved" (Acts 4:12).

When Paul spoke of a helmet for protection he, no doubt, was thinking of the necessity to protect the mind. Since Satan operates against the mind with enemy suggestions and worldly influence to accomplish his fiendish purposes, it must be protected. A person guarding his mind does not have to be what the world terms "closed-minded." A guarded Christian is not naive or uninformed. He is one who discerns right from wrong, and chooses that which is right. And he realizes the source of right action is right thinking, so he places himself in spheres of positive influence. Though he may come in contact with evil influences, he does not feast upon them. He does not allow them to become part of his mind-set. Evil does not shock him but it definitely disturbs him to the point of doing something about it.

How can we protect our minds from the evil one's influence? The following are four "guards" we need to put on duty.

1. Guard against negative thinking. Negative and faulty thinking can lead to depression. Bitterness and criticism add fuel to emotional discouragement until hopelessness develops and Satan has us right where he wants us. We become unable to help ourselves or others. Negativism is like a contagious disease. Listening to it for any length of time at all will allow it to latch onto us and eventually cause us powerlessness and defeat.

2. Guard against anything that makes sin acceptable. Some modern television programs, books, and magazines put sin in a fashionable light. "Everybody is doing it" seems to somehow translate into "I should be doing it," whether it is right or wrong. Adultery and

fornication are viewed as acceptable to an "enlight-ened age." We may at times be willing to call these things problems, but somehow we fail to see them as sin.

Teenagers especially are made to feel that they are missing something or that they are not "with it" if they don't participate in sinful activity. In fact, the world currently has an all-out campaign advertising sin. Yet the church often fails to see the problem and even shares the world's attitudes, views, and opinions (James 4:4).

3. Guard against fantasizing sin. Jesus made it clear when he said, "But I tell you that anyone who looks on a woman lustfully has already committed adultery with her in his heart" (Matt. 5:28). Pornography has become a blight to our nation. It has become a main avenue through which sensual sin has manifested it-self. The result is rape, divorce, depravity, and child abuse.

One way pornography destroys is through com-parisons. One's spouse will never measure up to the portrayal of the ultimate. A loving sense of helping each other through life is destroyed by a selfishness that seeks the "perfect 10." Pornography can produce the crack that will eventually cause a marriage to split.

4. Guard against anything that seeks to control your mind. Horoscopes, cult materials, and nonscriptural forms of meditation may seem harmless, but they abound with satanic activity. Such things usually breed fear and superstition. Avoid them as you would avoid anything that threatens your relationship with God.

The Sword of the Spirit. The sword of the spirit is God's Word. It is God's time-honored promise that he will bring us knowledge of the truth. It is both a defensive and an offensive weapon. "The Word of God is living and active. Sharper than any double-edged sword, it penetrates even to dividing soul and spirit, joints and marrow; it judges the thoughts and attitudes of the heart" (Heb. 4:12). We can ward off the enemy with it. When our minds come under assault, the Word—quoted, heard, or read—is capable of stopping the attack. Learn to find Scripture to fit the situation, then use it boldly. Speak it forth from your lips, directing it specifically at the problem you face. For example:

If you fear, quote 2 Timothy 1:7;

If you are worried, read Matthew 6:25-34;

If you are in financial trouble, note Philippians 4:19;

When you sin, remember 1 John 1:9;

When you need strength, read Isaiah 40:31;

When temptation strikes, quote Romans 8:37;

When you are unhappy, consider Nehemiah 8:10.

Paul ends his description of the armor of God with these words: "Pray in the Spirit on all occasions with all kinds of prayers and requests" (Eph. 6:18). Prayer is the means by which we get our training in warfare, as you will see when we talk about prayer in chapter 12.

But first we must talk about some areas of subtle attack, for you cannot fight the enemy effectively unless you recognize his strategy.

NOTES

1. Charles Swindoll, *Demonism* (Portland, Oreg.: Multnomah, 1981), 5.
2. Paul Billheimer, *Destined For the Throne* (Fort Washington, Penn.: Christian Literature Crusade, 1975), 98.
3. Ibid., 99.
4. Edmon C. Gruss, *Cults and the Occult* (Phillipsburg, N.J.: Presbyterian and Reformed, 1974), 143.
5. Jack W. Hayford, *Prayer Is Invading the Impossible* (Plainfield, N.J.: Logos International, 1977), 61.
6. Lloyd C. Douglas, *The Robe* (Boston: Houghton Mifflin, 1942), 342.
7. Andrew Murray, *With Christ in the School of Prayer* (Springdale, Penn.: Whitaker House, 1981), 97.

SEVEN

Overcoming the Attacks of the Enemy

My salvation experience began in my early teenage years. Not long afterward I began to encounter the work of the enemy. As it is with many new believers, my mind wrestled with a multitude of evil thoughts. Prior to the new birth experience I do not remember having trouble in this area. Then suddenly I had dozens of thoughts I did not want. In the usual pattern of such satanic oppression, there came the nagging suggestion that "if you were really a Christian you wouldn't think this way." Needless to say, when we fail to resist, discouragement comes and it is very easy to believe that we are the only ones experiencing such problems.

Though I did not want anyone to know what I was experiencing, I finally confessed the problem to my Christian grandfather. I was surprised to see that he understood, and it was then that I began to realize I was not alone. And something he said has helped immensely. "You can't stop the birds from flying over your head," he cautioned, "but you can keep them from making a nest in your hair." That wasn't original, but it began to help me as it had helped others. What Grandfather was saying was that you can't always stop the thought from coming, but you certainly do not need to entertain and feast on it. Furthermore, you do not need to feel guilty for thinking it in the first place. Simply realize that the thought wasn't yours and therefore do not accept responsibility for it.

There are many hindrances along the path of life that tend to slow us down in our quest to overcome. But when we realize how great the rewards are, we will see that any obstacle is worth working through.

It isn't always easy to determine whether a particular activity or influence is of the adversary or of the flesh. That is why we need the Holy Spirit's help in discerning which it is to keep from being deceived or even overcome. This discernment, coupled with a knowledge of the Word, makes it difficult for demons to carry out their schemes. Remember, we can only fight a battle if we know who our enemy is—the flesh or the devil.

Contrary to popular belief, everything that happens isn't necessarily a result of God's or Satan's control. Human nature and natural factors both have some effect on what takes place in this life. Unfortunately, there are Christians who believe that anything bad comes from demonic influence or activity. Illnesses, accidents, unfortunate happenings all come under the same heading: Demons. These people deny the possibility of natural weaknesses, illnesses, or temptations, even though Paul himself said that there are such things that are "common to all men." This mindset has led many into confusion and hurt their spiritual lives and witness.

While it is true that Satan's forces often work to activate our fleshly desires, we must recognize that control is available through Jesus Christ. We choose to submit either to the flesh or to the Holy Spirit. Day by day, perhaps moment by moment, we make decisions to live in the Spirit or in the flesh.

But beyond the temptations of the flesh we find problems with demon spirits. Before we get into the actual methods that demons use in their efforts to destroy us, we need to consider some of the different areas of attack. (Please note that problems in these areas are not always indicative of the working of evil spirits, and, furthermore, when demons are at work we are not released from personal responsibility for our actions and attitudes.

First, *they attack the physical body*. We all are under the earth's curse and, therefore, subject to its deteriorating effects upon our bodies. Slowly but surely these bodies wear out. But that is not the only problem our bodies face. From Scripture we know that evil spirits can directly affect us physically: "Then should not this woman, a daughter of Abraham, whom Satan has kept bound for eighteen long years, be set free on the Sabbath day from what bound her?" (Luke 13:16). Here was a woman who had been "crippled by a spirit" (v. 11). She was bent over and could not straighten up because of a demon. But the words of Jesus brought instant deliverance so that she was once again made whole.

Not every physical malady is of Satan. Some are caused by demons, some are the result of sin—both sin in the world and our own personal sin. (See Matt. 9:32-33; 12:22; and Mark 9:25 for information on spirits of dumbness, deafness, and blindness.)

Second, *demons attack the soul*. Psychological and moral problems often are the result of their heinous work. Those who understand spiritual warfare know that most of the work of the enemy actually begins in the soul, the seat of the will, mind, and emotions. From there demon spirits endeavor to spread their influence to the body in one direction and to the spirit in the other. In fact, doctors today confirm that a great percentage of human ills are psychosomatic, which means that the difficulty actually started in the soul realm. Wrong thinking, hatred, bitterness, negativism, and criticism all cause physical problems. In addition, when the mind is "tossed back and forth by the waves, and blown here and there by teaching" (Eph. 4:14) many spiritual problems can develop.

Our souls will continue to be an enormous playground for demon spirits if we do not claim protection by the Spirit of Christ. Our whole thinking and reasoning processes can be attacked, causing emotional distresses that fan out to create a vast host of other problems.

One of the enemy's most powerful attacks upon the mind is in the area of fantasizing. I'm not speaking of creative thought, remembering, planning, or even daydreaming, but rather of allowing the mind to be controlled by evil thoughts that pull a person into the realm of the flesh. Thoughts of illicit sex, murder, and violence may forcefully occupy the minds of many who have not taken on the protection of the Holy Spirit through the Word of God. These thoughts seem so close to reality that some people actually live a great portion of their lives in this make-believe, mind-controlled world. Others experience such heavy fear over these powerful thought processes that they often feel forced to actually do in deed what first began in the mind.

Paul tells the Romans that some people have actually gone so far in their evil thinking that they have pushed God out of their knowledge, and so God has given them "over to a depraved mind, to do what ought not to be done" (Rom 1:28). As a result, such evil thoughts can create a variety of psychological disorders: depression, fear, anxiety, guilt, jealousy, and hatred. All these are part of Satan's plan to destroy the human mind. The cure, of course, is to follow God's plan for restoration:

the renewing of the mind (Rom. 12:2; Eph. 4:23).

Third, *demons attack the human spirit.* When demons enter the human spirit they are, for all practical purposes, in full control of the individual involved. Here at the very core of human existence they render a person largely incapable of determining his own direction. A person controlled in his spirit is said to be "demon possessed." Demons then work out their own nefarious schemes through this person's mind and body. (Later in this chapter I will discuss demon possession in detail.)

The only defense against becoming demon possessed, or more accurately, "demon influenced," is to open the door of our spirit to Christ (Col. 1:27). The Spirit of Christ and demon spirits cannot possess us at the same time. But Satan works hard to keep Christ out. He sends seducing spirits with antichrist doctrines to confuse our minds and make it difficult to understand the simplicity of salvation through Jesus (2 Cor. 11:3; 1 Tim. 4:1).

Demons do not want us to know that Christ, by his Spirit, will live in our human spirits if we allow him in. When our spirits are filled with Jesus it is impossible for demons to gain entrance. When we accept Christ we literally invite him to take up residence within us. This does not mean that we as Christians will not be subject to satanic influence in the realm of our souls. Attacks against a believer's mind, if not properly countered by the Word of God with the help of the Holy Spirit, may even result in some kind of control by a demon—it amounts to a kind of brainwashing. This does not mean that such a person is possessed in the same sense as when a demon is either in partial or full control of an unbeliever's spirit. It means that the demon is exerting such strong influence that the person involved is acting inappropriately. It is the new nature of Christ at work in the believer's spirit that eventually alerts him to the presence of the demon and then helps him to resist until literally all influence is gone.

A SUBTLE ATTACK

While it is quite true that much of what is about to be described is the result of our own flesh, demons, nevertheless, do everything possible to heighten problems in these areas because they know the damage that can be done. The only solution for an unbeliever is to accept Christ as Savior and Lord. Then through Jesus certain procedures are learned that protect from demonic attack.

One solution for a Christian is periodic examination (2 Cor. 13:5). Such examination, with God's help, will reveal areas where the body senses are not under the control of the spirit, thus resulting in fleshly actions. It also will reveal areas where Satan is working, areas that can be overcome by resisting. James says, "Submit yourselves, then, to God. Resist the devil, and he will flee from you" (James 4:7).

Personal examination is important, but too much introspection, especially by sensitive Christians, can be dangerous. We need to ask God from time to time if there are things in our lives that should not be there. But we should never become fearful that we have missed something when we have searched for it diligently. It is unhealthy to think that God is going to reject us because of some hidden thing we ourselves are not able to find. Some people, obsessed with fear and overcome with agony, have wondered if God is going to turn his back on them because they have not yet found everything that must be changed. Satan uses this trick to immobilize them by fear and thus render them ineffective in their lives for God. To guard against this, we need to have an understanding of grace and justification in Jesus. We also need to go before God and ask him to help us discover anything that will hinder full fellowship with him, and trust him to honor our request. He will not let us down or leave a wrong unrevealed when we want to please him.

The following are some things that might be found upon personal examination. They are problems that deal with our own personal *will* but often are inspired by demons. They are parts of the subtle attack that can and must be conquered for us to be effective in overcoming.

Lukewarmness. An indifferent spirit in a Christian indicates that the person's interests do not lie in the things of Christ. Believers who are lukewarm have left their first love (Rev. 2:4).

Those who are lukewarm may become quite lackadaisical in their approach to eternal matters. Their state of inaction gives the appearance of spiritual drowsiness or sleepiness. Proverbs would call such people sluggards: "Take a lesson from the ants you lazy fellow. Learn from their ways and be wise! For though they have no king to make them work, yet they labor hard all summer, gathering food for the winter. But you—all you do is sleep. When will you wake up? 'Let me sleep a little longer!' Sure, just a little more! And as you sleep, poverty creeps upon you like a robber and destroys you; want attacks you in full armor" (Prov. 6:6-11, TLB).

People who are lukewarm do not include prayer, Bible study, or fellowship in their highest priorities. Rather, self and materialistic things top the list.

Christ's words to such people are most disturbing. "Because you are lukewarm—neither hot nor cold—I am about to spit you out of my mouth" (Rev. 3:16). That sounds rather cold and almost callous. But it's not! The Lord knows that many other soldiers can be adversely affected by the laziness and lethargy of one person or group of people.

The Cares of Life. Affluence and misplaced priorities concerning the cares of this life can contribute greatly to a lukewarm attitude and cause "unfruitfulness" (Matt. 13:22). Of course, being wealthy is not a sin. But the way one uses wealth can be a sin. Paul tells Timothy to admonish those who are rich "not to be arrogant nor to put their hope in wealth, which is so uncertain, but to put their hope in God, who richly provides us with everything for our enjoyment" (1 Tim. 6:17).

The basic problem with riches is covetousness. When you seek power, security, and happiness through finances, you are using wealth to try to satisfy an inner need that only Jesus Christ can fill. Coveting money is a serious matter. "People who want to get rich fall into temptation and a trap and into many foolish and harmful desires that plunge men into ruin and destruction. For the love of money is a root of all kinds of evil. Some people, eager for money, have wandered from the faith and pierced themselves with many griefs" (1 Tim. 6:9-10).

Beloved Christian, be very careful with the idea that once you reach financial security you will be free to serve the Lord unhindered. God never has and never will work that way. When he calls he works out the finances according to his desire, thus proving his ability to sustain. Do not be tempted to point to unwise religious fanaticism that has resulted in financial ruin for some people as an excuse for taking matters into your own hands. One person's foolishness does not excuse another's faithlessness.

Busyness. Well thought-out plans by a settled heart provide great gain and a sense of fulfillment. But those with anxious spirits may accomplish very little and therefore must stay constantly busy in order to feel fulfilled. They may have a few significant achievements, but that doesn't matter for they find satisfaction in constant movement. Eventually, such "motion without meaning" catches up with them when they are forced to look back and see nothing but wood, hay, and stubble where they should see gold, silver, and precious stones (1 Cor. 3:12). Had they spent time waiting on God for direction and rested spirits, their lives would have had greater effect (Ps. 37:7).

Unjustified Ignorance. A spirit of "I won't" rather than "I honestly am not able" often characterizes people who are destitute of knowledge. They are ignorant by choice and not by ability. To some, being uninformed is a matter of being uninstructed, and a lack of instruction is quite often a matter of laziness. Lack of teachableness—being unwilling to learn—also contributes to the problem.

Some have the idea that to be uninformed means they will not be held accountable for what they do or do not do. They reason, "How can God judge me for things of which I am ignorant?" These people, no doubt, will be judged the most severely. Having the Word of God available and rejecting it on the basis of this logic is a horrendous crime. This attitude approaches that of the apostates who have decided not to "retain the knowledge of God" (Rom. 1:28).

Unfaithfulness. In Matthew 24, where Jesus speaks of his second coming, he mentions a condition that would exist in the last days because of the increase of wickedness. He says, "The love of most will grow cold" (v. 12). Nothing damages a relationship like the loss of love. When love goes, care, respect, admiration, concern, attention, and courtesy all go right along with it. Perhaps more accurately we should say that when these things (care, respect, admiration, etc.) go, then love also goes. For these things are the very roots of love. When they are gone, all that is left to fill the void is neglect, unconcern, hatred, and disrespect.

Allegiances are forsaken, vows are broken, duty is disregarded, confidence is destroyed, dishonesty sets in, and a relationship is shattered . . . all because someone ignored commitments and allowed selfishness to rule. Where once loyalty dictated action, now animosity allows inaction. Where once there was response to others, now there is coldness and indifference. And no response means no relationship.

Negative emotions can play a huge part in this whole scene. We can quickly smother devotion if our allegiance is based on feeling. It is here that commitment becomes important. Commitment says, "I will live up to my part of the bargain. I will not allow feelings, emotions, or circumstances to hinder me from doing my best to fulfill the agreement."

Without question, discipline plays a great part in faithfulness to relationships. We must learn to discipline ourselves in the little things of life first, for a little neglect today can bring major disaster tomorrow. "Whoever can be trusted with very little can also be trusted with much, and whoever is dishonest with very little will also be dishonest with much" (Luke 16:10). Some good starting places are being on time wherever you go; honoring your word—when you say you will do something, do it; and developing good habits of prayer, Bible study, and fellowship.

Compromise. The usual excuse for doing what we want to do—whether it's right or wrong—is often, "Everybody else is doing it." What is ethically or morally wrong seems to make little difference as long as we can find others who are doing what we want to do.

The human conscience that is not in tune with God's Word justifies evil in the sight of evil. In other words, it is easier to do wrong when we ourselves are watching it being done.

When Paul wrote his second letter to the Corinthians, he identified those who apparently used other people as a yardstick for their own spirituality. "We do not dare to classify or compare ourselves with some who commend themselves. When they measure themselves by themselves and compare themselves with themselves, they are not wise" (2 Cor. 10:12).

Another compromise we make is in the area of retribution. It's the "eye for an eye" mentality. "I can cheat on my income tax because the government is already crooked." "It's OK to keep the extra money a cashier gives me by mistake because stores rip me off with high prices anyway." "She isn't what I wanted in a wife, so I think I should be able to make up for it by seeing other women."

If we want God's best, and if we want to escape judgment, we must honor his Word regardless of the situation. And yet in countless cases, especially concerning marriage and divorce, there seems no end to unscriptural compromise. The Scripture is clear that a believer is not to marry an unbeliever. But many insist upon it anyway and for any number of reasons: "I'll lead him to the Lord." "He is a wonderful person. In fact, he's better than most Christians I know." On and on the excuses go as believers whose Father is God often insist on marrying people whose father is the devil. In essence, that makes Satan those Christians' father-in-law—and that means the enemy has a legal right to enter their homes.

There are those who will always try to vindicate their corrupt actions for a variety of reasons—all selfish. James says, "Anyone, then, who knows the good he ought to do and doesn't do it, sins" (James 4:17). God expects our every activity to be measured by his Word.

These are but a few of the types of attacks that seem small and negligible, but that can subtly lead us into bondage.

A POWERFUL ATTACK

Many of the following areas of conflict have their source in either the flesh or demons, or both. Though we will deal mostly with problems of demonic origin, it frequently becomes important to deal first with the physical, emotional, mental, and spiritual problems. Though these problems may originally have had nothing to do with the enemy, they can become staging areas for evil deployment, for when demons see a problem arising they take advantage of it.

Depression. Depression can be described simply as a low spirit. Basically it is a problem with the human spirit, even though it may be experienced in the soul as feelings of despair and in the body as sensations that tend to go beyond normal fatigue.

There is not enough room here to fully describe the tremendously adverse effects depression can have on a person's total being. For this reason, I recommend that those suffering from this malady not take it lightly but rather research the subject through good literature or, if necessary, get professional help. There is nothing wrong with seeking Christian doctors, counselors, and pastors who use God's Word as their source of authority to help overcome the effects of depression. We fulfill the law of Christ by bearing one another's burdens (Gal. 6:2).

Depression can be psychological or physical in origin as well as spiritual, but it's hard to tell these apart since aspects of all three often are involved. Spiritual depression can result from feelings of guilt or anger, misunderstanding God's Word, perceiving a situation incorrectly, or even a direct attack by Satan. Psychological depression can be caused by emotional turmoil such as the death of a loved one. Physical depression can result from many things including chemical imbalances, lack of rest or sleep, or sicknesses.

Satanic inspired depression usually comes as a result of an attack on the mind. Demonic thoughts that are not properly resisted tend to bring the spirit low. This is especially true in people who are not already strong in spirit and who are not aware of how Satan works in this manner.

What things can Satan's demons use against us to bring on depression?

First, loss and the fear of loss can bring on depression. The loss of a loved one, of a job, of self-esteem, of health, of a friendship, of family unity—virtually any kind of loss may cause depression. Simply being aware of our vulnerability during these times of crisis allows us to defend ourselves against mental misery. It also helps us know when to give aid to others in order to keep them from being overcome with this inner pain. Whenever a brother or sister in Christ suffers a significant loss, we should prayerfully recognize our responsibility to give immediate ministry.

Second, Satan uses inappropriately suppressed anger to bring on depression. Some of our emotions can and even should be rejected. We do not always need to act out or express our anger. But hidden anger can be the source of many deep emotional problems. It is probably a greater cause of depression among Christians than among nonbelievers. Christians sometimes have the mistaken idea that it is a sin to be angry. Yet Scripture says, "In your anger do not sin" (Eph. 4:26). This indicates that if we handle anger in a proper way—not suppressing it until it forces its way out in some undesirable manner—it is an emotion that is approved of by God.

Jesus became very angry at times. On one occasion he "overturned the table of the money changers" because they were making God's house of prayer a den of robbers (Matt. 21:12-13).

But many of us have trouble expressing anger without sinning in the process. When it is properly expressed, anger should not inspire "hatred, discord, jealousy, fits of rage" (Gal. 5:20). Also, note that Paul tells us not to "let the sun go down while you are still angry" (Eph. 4:26). In other words, don't go to bed upset.

Third, unfulfilled expectations often trigger depression. Many, if not all of us, have had our hearts set on something that we didn't get. And we know how it feels to have a dream fizzle over the years. It is natural to have many hopes, desires, and plans that we believe will make us happy. But sometimes we strive after them so intently that when they fail to materialize, we tend to fall in spirit. There isn't a thing wrong with utilizing good plans and realistic dreams. These, however, should never be the source of our hope. Only Christ can fill that place in the human heart. He and he alone is to be our hope. When we understand this, we can go ahead and desire and plan with the attitude that "if it is the Lord's will, we will live and do this or that" (James 4:15). If what we desire comes to pass we can say "Praise the Lord." If it doesn't, we can continue to say "Praise the Lord" because we know that God still delights in giving good things to his children and that he will do so later if we wait (Isa. 40:31; Matt. 7:11; James 1:17).

Fourth, negativism can cause depression. Negativism is an extremely dangerous attitude because it is a basis for hopelessness. It destroys faith and happiness and refuses the gift of love. It enhances rebellion and promotes deception; people have been tempted to take sides and give up allegiances all because someone spoke negatively. People motivated by negativism often have no grounds for their decisions; they move on emotions alone. It doesn't take long for such negativism to reduce the spirit to heavy bouts of depression. Some people seem to thrive on the destruction brought about by the negative comments of the human tongue.

One of the best gifts God gives to the redeemed is the inner caution to stay away from a person with a negative spirit. In Christ we become encouraged to check out all sides of a given situation before making an evaluation. God moves in our hearts to help us see the best in everything instead of the worst. A positive attitude allows God to fulfill Romans 8:28 in us on a regular basis: "And we know that in all things God works for the good of those who love him, who have been called according to his purpose."

Fifth, low self-esteem often leads to self-pity which in turn leads to depression. And along the way negativism and suppressed anger usually are picked up, making the weight of depression unbearable.

The self-centered life seems to have lots of glamour and glitter, but it never has any substance. It screams the loudest and offers the most, but it never pays off. It claims to be the real you, but it isn't even close to what God created you to be. It is one of the deepest and ugliest aspects of rebellion; it is the part of man to which Satan offers deification in order to capture his attention and then his loyalty.

Evil spirits work to resurrect our old nature with all of its old ways. Satan tempts us with the belief that we deserve something better in life. But we need not give in to a selfish spirit; we must not let it affect or inhabit our thinking. Jesus tells us that only death to self will bring about new life: "Unless a kernel of wheat falls to the ground and dies, it remains only a single seed. But if it dies, it produces many seeds" (John 12:24).

Fear. Although fear is basically a lack of trust, it also can be defined as "an emotional response to a potentially harmful set of circumstances that we think are beyond our control." This unnatural and dangerous kind of fear is not what the Scriptures refer to in verses such as: "Love the brotherhood of believers, fear God, honor the king" (1 Pet. 2:17). To fear God means to respect him.

The fear that comes from the enemy is best described as anxiety. Satan delights in scare tactics. He loves for us to be unsettled in spirit because that can keep us from finding inner peace through a love relationship with God.

To be careful around poisonous snakes and fire because we recognize the danger they represent is a good thing. But to be constantly harassed in mind, thinking that either one is about to do us harm when neither one is present, is an inordinate fear. It is this kind of fear that binds many people. It is fear where there is no need to fear.

Many times in Scripture we find the expression "fear not." Proverbs says, "Have no fear of sudden disaster" (Prov. 3:25). This binding type of fear comes so strongly to some that they are overwhelmed by it. It is a condition of fright and causes extreme emotional distress. It is well known that there are hundreds of so-called phobias that affect people throughout the world. For Christians, phobias become a serious danger when they are allowed to grow so powerful that they actually seem bigger than God's power to intervene. When this happens, the believer's faith becomes misdirected.

We know that inner terror, panic, and alarm do not

come from God for we are assured that "there is no fear in love. But perfect love drives out fear, because fear has to do with punishment. The man who fears is not made perfect in love" (1 John 4:18). John goes on to say that we love God because he first loved us. God's love shown through his Word and by his Spirit will always replace tormenting fear with wonderful peace.

What God told Israel through Isaiah about fear is still true for his people today: "Do not fear, for I am with you; do not be dismayed, for I am your God. I will strengthen you and will help you; I will uphold you with my righteous right hand" (Isa. 41:10). God's marvelous love through Christ makes it possible to overcome the fear of: man (Luke 12:4-5); death (Heb. 2:15); the future (Luke 21:26); danger (Gen. 46:3); evil (Ps. 23:4); war (Ps. 27:3); enemies (Ps. 118:5-6); and any other fears that may come our way.

There is a story of a young boy who came running through the back door of his home yelling, "Mommy, mommy, there's a great big lion in our back yard." His mother looked out the window just in time to see a big yellow dog jump the fence. Turning to her son she said, "Johnny, I've told you over and over you are not to lie to me and you've just told another big lie. You go to your bedroom and tell God that you are sorry for lying." So little Johnny went off to his room. After a time he came back into the kitchen. His mother looked down at him and asked, "Son, did you tell God that you were sorry for lying?" "Yes," the boy replied, "but he told me not to worry. He said the first time he saw that big yellow dog he thought it was a lion too."

As humorous as that story might be, it shows that there are a lot of problems in life that seem terrifying, but are no more than "big yellow dogs." And we need to invite these problems to "jump the fence."

Also, since worry is just another form of fear, we need to note Matthew 6:25 where Jesus commands us not to worry: "Therefore I tell you, do not worry about your life, what you will eat or drink; or about your body, what you will wear. Is not life more important than food, and the body more important than clothes?"

Hatred. Violent dislike and animosity—a desire to destroy—characterize a person overcome by a spirit of hatred. So deadly is this enemy spirit that it not only affects the hated, but the hater as well. In fact, the Bible equates hatred with murder: "Anyone who hates his brother is a murderer, and you know that no murderer has eternal life in him" (1 John 3:15). Hatred can literally kill the person it is aimed at and can keep the one harboring the hate from eternal life. "That's a little strong," you might say. But it is God's Word that makes this powerful statement. Still, many people take God's caution quite lightly and allow coolness, enmity, hostility, resentment, bitterness, and even rage to occupy the center of their existence. They don't realize the damage these things are doing. There also are those who allow their animosity to reach the point that they actually wish harm and even death on the person they hate.

How does hatred kill? Foremost, it causes stress—the kind of stress that affects the different biological systems within the body. This upset can put such undue pressures on certain physical functions that there is a collapse and the person dies. This connection between the hate-induced stress and the death is seldom recognized because it is not immediate. The result may be seen only as a shortened life span. However, though the hatred may not end in death for some twenty, thirty, or even forty years, God still calls it murder.

The medical world in recent years has become increasingly aware of the potential damage inner attitudes and emotions can cause to the physical body. It is estimated that psychosomatic disorders account for up to 85 percent of what is wrong with the human body. That doesn't mean that taking a placebo will make the problem go away. But it does mean that the way a person thinks can cause a real physical ailment. Is it, then, any wonder that demon spirits work so hard to affect a person's mind and fill it with hatred and un-forgiveness?

Those who allow themselves to harbor hatred are generally those who suffer the most severe emotional pain. The acid of bitterness slowly begins to eat the heart out. In Matthew's Gospel, Jesus tells of a man who refused to forgive and how he was therefore turned over to the tormentors (Matthew 18:34). This certainly seems to be the case with many today who, because of their inner animosity, experience a great deal of mental torment.

Jesus Christ came bearing a message of love and forgiveness, a message that would not only extend physical life, but provide eternal life as well. So moved was the Apostle John with this tremendous love of God and its benefits that it was the theme of much of his writing (as we can see, for example, in 1 John). And in God's Word we see, time and again, that the love of God not only casts out fear, but it will cast out hatred as well.

Guilt. There is a kind of guilt that comes from God, that is associated with what we generally call "conviction," which simply means "to be convinced." It is a sense deep within the human spirit that an error has been or is about to be committed. It is a kind of early warning device designed to bring about a mid-course correction. Failure to yield to this voice within the human conscience allows sin to be committed and usually brings on feelings of remorse, regret, and sorrow. Conviction is found in the spirit. It is an inner "knowing" concerning right and wrong.

Guilt, however, is centered in the soul. It is the feelings and emotions generated from knowing that God or someone else is upset with our actions. And it is good that we are sensitive to these things, otherwise we would not respond properly to right and wrong. Instead, we would soon experience the disastrous effects of our wayward actions. God has created this as a system to keep us out of trouble.

But in order to operate effectively in this system, we must understand God's grace in forgiveness and turn from wrongdoing when the warning light of conviction and guilt goes on. If we fail to turn at repeated warnings we will become insensitive and our consciences will become seared as if with a hot iron (1 Tim. 4:2). But if we confess our sins and receive God's love, we can walk on as if nothing had happened. That's grace, wondrous grace. The best way to confess is to get alone with God and tell him audibly of the mistakes you have made. Don't develop the attitude that he knows you're sorry so you really don't have to say anything to him.

Satan seizes on our emotional disturbances when we commit sin and endeavors to keep love and forgiveness from blotting out the offense. He does everything he can to make us continue to feel bad until all hope and peace of mind seem gone. Then feelings of despair, worthlessness, and uselessness will come until it becomes nearly impossible for us to see ourselves in Christ and seated with him in heavenly places. And the demons know all too well that it is difficult for Christ to work in us when we are in this condition.

Another ploy very similar to the one just mentioned occurs when we ask for forgiveness and, for a while, "feel" all right. But later, especially when God wants to move us onward to maturity, we encounter tremendous guilt all over again for what we have already turned over to the Lord. This is false guilt, and it is yet an-

154

other ploy of the enemy. If we do not recognize this tactic and immediately begin to resist on the basis that the particular account is already settled because we've confessed it, Satan will run us around in circles, cause us all kinds of emotional problems, and make us ineffective as soldiers of the Cross.

Guilt is also possible as a result of suggestions of others. The judgments of others have a deep effect upon us.

Inferiority. Feelings of low self-esteem are natural and warranted for all of mankind because of the Fall. Because we are sinful and at enmity with God, none of us is righteous, not a single person (Rom. 3:10). Therefore feeling bad is normal. It also means that all our righteousness (self-righteousness) is like filthy rags in God's sight (Isa. 64:6). That's the bottom line.

We have reason to feel inferior to the model of perfection as Scripture describes it because we *are* inferior. Usually, if we are afraid that others may find out what we are really like, it is because we know that we really do have something to hide.

Humanistic psychology, however, tries to hide our problems behind a bigger fig leaf. But it fails us drastically in finding solutions to our problems by not dealing with the real problem—sin. Humanism uses the doctrines of demons to hold us up or to allow us to be puffed up for a time. Then, when we are finally let down, we lose all hope. Humanism says we are all right when we are not. Pride may keep us afloat for awhile, but eventually we have to face our true horrible selves—something no man can do without Christ.

Fortunately, because of the sacrifice of Calvary, God no longer looks at us the way we are. He looks at us through Jesus. With the Spirit of Christ living within, we become new creations in him. Old sinful things pass away, replaced by new deeds of true righteousness (2 Cor. 5:17). God literally imputes righteousness into us when we believe in and receive Christ as Lord and Savior (Rom. 4:5-7). This causes us to become brand new people. Now old feelings of inferiority can go. We're King's kids about to inherit the universe with Jesus. We are being justified. We are being sanctified. We are freed from sin. We need not feel bad, guilty, or sinful. We need only recognize who we are now and what our present position is with God: and then rejoice (Eph. 2:4-7)! Oh, it's true we still fail from time to time, but God sees us in Christ and therefore still regards us as his own. Repentance allows us to once again find justification.

God is not interested in helping us feel better about ourselves. He does not want our attention in any way turned inward. To be turned in that direction only produces other potential problems with sin—especially sin involving pride and self-centeredness. What God wants is our attention placed on him and on others. He knows this is the only way to truly solve the problem of inferiority. He also wants all aspects of guilt and low self-esteem removed. We tend to think that if we feel better about ourselves we won't feel bad. Not so. First of all, feelings are only there for the moment. They will not last because they are not of the spirit. Second, "better" is a degree. What degree of "better" does it take for us to feel fulfilled? Will we need to feel a better "better" tomorrow than the better we felt today? You see, the whole matter becomes very subjective. That's why this kind of introspection is dangerous.

The happiness that comes from not always being saddled with the weight of feelings about ourselves is indescribable. Not having to contend with proving ourselves, especially to ourselves, is a great relief.

When we constantly wonder if we are good enough, we often waste time over matters that are not to concern us. This does not mean that we will not need to periodically examine ourselves as Scripture exhorts us to do. It means that we are not to grow anxious or worry over such matters. Since Christ has become our righteousness, all we need to concern ourselves with is a walk in the Spirit. Such a walk causes us to perceive in our spirits that everything between us and God is all right. And that is a wonderful contentment to have as we sing, *It is well with my soul.*

Discouragement. Discouragement means to be without courage. Such is the condition when hope seems gone. It puts heavy pressure on the spirit and brings the soul into disarray.

An unknown writer describes how the devil uses discouragement to impoverish the spirit:

> It was announced that the devil was going out of business and would offer all his tools for sale to whoever would pay the price. On the night of the sale they were all attractively displayed: Malice, Hatred, Envy, Jealousy, Sensuality, and Deceit among them. Each was marked with its own price.
>
> To the side lay a harmless-looking wedge-shaped tool, much more worn and priced higher than any of the others.
>
> Someone asked the devil what it was.
>
> "That's Discouragement," was the reply.
>
> "Why do you have it priced so high?"
>
> "Because," replied the devil, "it is more useful to me than any of the others. I can pry open and get inside of a man's consciousness with that when I could never get near him with any of the others."

Satan often uses the circumstances of life to discourage us. He did it with David in the Bible. David and his men were away from their encampment when the Amalekites invaded and captured all the women and children. When David and his men returned they were met with tremendous discouragement. They had no idea of the welfare of their loved ones. Not only was David himself distressed, but his men were now talking of stoning him. David could have collapsed under the weight of discouragement. But he didn't. Instead, he began to solve his problem first in spirit. Scripture says, "But David found strength in the Lord his God" (1 Sam. 30:6). Next he turned to God for direction. The end of the matter was that "David recovered everything the Amalekites had taken" (1 Sam. 30:18). David's victory began when he refused to accept defeat in his spirit.

The psalmist writes, "Be strong and take heart, all you who hope in the Lord" (Ps. 31:24). Again the psalmist approaches the subject, "Why are you downcast, O my soul? Why so disturbed within me? Put your hope in God for I will yet praise him, my Savior and my God" (Ps. 43:5).

AN OVERWHELMING ATTACK—
DEMON POSSESSION

That men can be possessed of demon spirits is evident from Scripture (see Matt. 4:24; 8:16, 28-34; 9:32-34; 10:1, 8; 12:22, 43-45; 15:22-28; 17:14-21).

Perhaps one of the greatest areas of misunderstanding and misinformation within the Church of Jesus Christ today lies in this area of demon control. Few have taken the time or the energy to adequately research this realm in order to speak knowledgeably on it; some perhaps because they were attacked themselves when they endeavored to do so, some because of fear, others because they never really had an interest or saw a need. Whatever the reason, one fact still remains: there is a great deal of ignorance when it comes to these deepest of enemy workings—demon possession and demon oppression. Basically, when a person is demon-possessed, the demon has gained overwhelming control in that person's spirit. When someone is being oppressed by a demon, that means the demon is waging a war against the person through temptation and outside suggestions or influences. This is accomplished in the mind.

For our study, let's begin with the word *possession* and its subsequent meaning. The Greek word for possession is *daimonizomai* (demonized), which means to "have or be vexed with a devil." The word *possessed* gives the idea that the person involved belongs to a demon or demons. However, this is a mistaken impression because demons cannot possess anything. In fact, since they are created beings, they themselves are owned by God, the Creator. And they will be judged by God as well. So what we call demon "possession" is, in reality, more like demon "encroachment" or "intrusion." They invade; they do not own.

Perhaps the best explanation of possession comes from the idea of overwhelming influence. Differing degrees of influence show the difference between possession and oppression. *Possession* identifies the strong influence of a demon that has gone past the realm of the soul and has entered into the human spirit of an unbeliever. *Oppression* is a strong influence only on the soul, and it can affect believer and unbeliever alike.

Let's examine, then, the areas of influence and possession in light of our study on the body, soul, and spirit. If the spirit of man is seen as his inner "holy of holies" (the residence of the real person housed in a body of flesh and bones and given a soul to relate both to a material world and a spiritual world), then within that inner sanctuary it would be impossible for God and demons to dwell together. If demons are found dwelling in this realm, they are intent on bringing the person involved to total ruin. If God is allowed to dwell there, he is intent on establishing wholeness and completeness. These are two vastly different goals from two opposing realms.

When demons enter a person's spirit we generally say that the person is "possessed." What has actually happened is that the demon or demons have gained such powerful influence that the person is almost completely controlled by the enemy. In most cases the person is allowed a degree of normalcy, which keeps other people from realizing that he or she has a problem in this area. If, however, Christ lives in a person's spirit, demon possession isn't possible. But, unfortunately, demon influence is! Demons find occasion to work against Christians through the realm of their souls—through the will, mind, and emotions. And they are capable of doing so even if Christ has entered the spirit of the person. Since Christ never operates by force, we become responsible for what takes place in the realm of the soul. It is here that we must choose to submit to the Lordship of Jesus Christ, to actively enter the warfare against the devil, to deny sin, and to be obedient to God's Word. In doing these things we combat the work of the enemy against our souls.

Many Christians today are in need of deliverance from the influence of demons. In certain cases, the influence is so strong that some believers even appear to be possessed. They have allowed the enemy to work in their souls. Although Christ still lives in the believers' spirits, demons can work through their souls and do to them many of the things they do to unbelievers. This is why it is so important to resist the enemy. When we discover him working in our minds, we need not worry about the semantics of possession, oppression, influence, etc. We need simply to resist him. When he moves in our emotions, trying to make us psychological wrecks, we need to resist him. When we are tempted to allow hostility, resentment, or animosity to govern, again the key is resistance. In severe cases, some Christians may find it necessary for other believers to help them bind and break the powers of the enemy through intercessory prayer.

How can we recognize the presence of demons, especially in unbelievers? C. Fred Dickason describes it this way:

> Symptoms may seem to overlap with certain mental, emotional, or physical disorders, as they did in the Gospels. But symptoms such as unusual physical strength or intelligence, sudden changes and reverses in emotions, manifestations of another personality, continual blasphemous thoughts, and recurrent urges to harm or to commit suicide are possible signs of demonic presence (see Mark 5:1-20).
>
> Inability to trust God, pray, read the Bible, say the name of the Lord Jesus, and accept or hear spiritual truth are even more suspicious symptoms. So also are pressures or invisible attacks upon the body and appearances of dark figures. Mediumistic or clairvoyant powers, falling into trances, change of persons speaking, magical abilities, inserted or unwanted thoughts, and voices that attack God or the person all can be indicators of demonic activity.[1]

There are many cases today in which some "Christians" manifest the presence of demons. Others are shocked at what they see and so fail to do anything about it; their theology causes them to refuse to believe what is right before their eyes. These people need to consider Matthew 12:22-28 and 43-45, where Jesus discusses the reality of spirits both inhabiting and affecting people. In view of these and other Scriptures, it is impossible for us, as conscientious, thinking Christians, to say we believe in the Bible and Christ and yet deny the reality of demons and their works.

How do demons gain control? The following is a partial list of the methods the enemy uses to subdue people:

1. *Mind-altering substances such as drugs and alcohol.* These substances reduce a person's ability to resist demons and therefore grant the demons increasing influence.

2. *Mind-control teaching.* These teachings, especially the kinds that encourage passivity, blanking out the mind, and unquestioned devotion to an individual, provide an entrance point for demon activity.

3. *Participation in the occult.* This allows the enemy major degrees of control.

4. *The environment.* Influence can be gained when a person visits places where demon activity is abundant (i.e., rock concerts, bars, certain kinds of parties, and any other place where sinful activity is practiced).

5. *Family influence.* Certain kinds of demons appear to affect some families for generations.

6. *Fear.* This emotion seems to be an open door for demons in some people. A traumatic situation is sometimes an entrance point as well.

7. *Sinful habits.* To practice sin, especially known sin, grants the enemy a certain access.

8. *Defiance and rebellion.* Demon activity is often abundant wherever these attitudes exist.

What are some of the symptoms where there is strong demon activity? The following list represents certain manifestations of those who are demonized. (It is important to note, however, that doing the following things does not always mean a person is demonized.)

- Violent, uncontrolled behavior usually accompanied by incredible physical strength;
- Blasphemy;
- Immediate and abrupt behavior change when the name of Jesus is mentioned;
- Inability to say the name of Jesus (while the demon

may say the name of Jesus, it usually tries to prevent the person involved from doing so);
- Inability to control the desire for pornography, adultery, fornication, masturbation, and homosexuality;
- Strong compulsions toward suicide, murder, stealing, lying, and other forms of known sin;
- A driving force toward hatred, jealousy, backbiting, envy, pride, bitterness, negativism, and criticism.

It is easy to become disturbed by wondering if you yourself might have a demon. Many who think they do, don't, while many who are unaware of demons' existence are actually plagued by them. The first step in either case is not to be afraid. Next, begin to examine any behavior manifestation that is inappropriate or out of character. Then deal with that manifestation. By turning to Jesus and resisting the enemy, many if not all problems will cease. If this is not effective, Christ has given his people powerful ministry in deliverance. Certain people within the body of Christ have been given special abilities in order to break the chains of the enemy over possessed and oppressed individuals. Seek them out and ask for their intervention on your behalf.

To this point we have discussed some of the areas where, if we are not aware of his tactics, Satan works very effectively. In the next chapter we will examine an area of difficulty for which we often are not prepared: suffering and sorrow.

NOTES

1. C. Fred Dickason, "Demons Our Invisible Enemies," *Fundamentalist Journal*, October 1984, 23.

EIGHT

Overcoming in Suffering and Sorrow

The Manchester Guardian carried the following accident report submitted by a West Indies bricklayer to his supervisor:

> Asked to bring down some excess bricks from the third floor, the workman rigged up a beam and pulley, hoisted up a barrel, and tied it in place. After filling the barrel with bricks, he returned to the ground and untied the rope, intending to lower the barrel to the ground.
>
> Unfortunately, he had misjudged the weight of the bricks. As the barrel started down, it jerked him off the ground so fast and so far that he was afraid to let go. Halfway up, he met the barrel coming down and received a severe blow on the shoulder.
>
> "I then continued to the top," the bricklayer explained, "banging my head against the beam and getting my fingers jammed in the pulley. When the barrel hit the ground it burst its bottom, allowing the bricks to spill out. I was now heavier than the barrel and so I started down again at high speed.
>
> "Halfway down I met the barrel coming up and received severe injuries to my shins. When I hit the

ground I landed on the bricks, getting several painful cuts from the sharp edges.

"At this point I must have lost my presence of mind because I let go of the line. The barrel then came down, giving me another heavy blow on the head and putting me in the hospital.

"I respectfully request sick leave."

We generally don't have to travel too far in life before we meet with the struggles—the ups and downs. And as much as we may not want to believe it, suffering comes to sinner and saint alike. But struggles, temptations, and sorrows can have a positive effect if we approach them correctly.

Dick Reilly tells the story of a man in India who was forced to live in poverty because of his faith in Jesus. Though he came from a wealthy family, he was denied his inheritance because he believed the gospel message and followed Christ. When asked how he endured so much suffering this man said simply, "It is better to have a pain in the stomach than to have a pain in the heart."

Off and on through the centuries the Church has lived a much defeated life, giving more attention to the enemy than to victory in Jesus Christ. A gloom and doom attitude often has prevailed. Our century, especially in the last thirty years or so, has been no exception. Perhaps people developed this attitude after hearing sermons that emphasized the imminent return of the Lord. Such sermons, though scriptural in content, sometimes left those who heard them with a defeatist mentality. Many assumed that since the Bible foretold horrible things happening just prior to the return of Christ there was nothing anyone could do to forestall the wrath of God. And Christians were doomed to suffer right along with everyone else.

Then, more recently, the Holy Spirit illuminated portions of the Word that reveal that "in all these things we are more than conquerors through him who loved us" (Rom. 8:37). It was a message of victory and not defeat; a message of hope, not one that produces miserable, poverty-stricken, depressed, sorrowful, fear-filled lives.

This illumination was nothing more than the simple gospel message of the kingdom. Suddenly many who lived trampled lives were raised to wholeness; healings took place, bondages were broken, faith began to rise, and God was glorified. Almost overnight new excitement moved through much of the body of Christ. Suddenly, with victories and more in sight, proponents of an ideal Christian living came along. They stressed an abundance of peace, joy, happiness, material blessings, and perfect health without the slightest aspect of trouble. If problems did come, they asserted, faith would work a quick remedy and one could again go directly to "silver spoon" living. Everything depended on receiving miracles, and miracles came only through faith. And so faith became the primary message.

But as with so many other beautiful truths of God's Word, the faith message soon lost its balance and suffered staggering misconceptions. True, most Christians never discover all of their spiritual rights. And true, God loves to work miracles among his people. But much of the faith message left out crucial spiritual truths, and instead of liberating a person for abundant living it brought another kind of bondage. Some people, no matter how hard they believed or tried to believe and no matter how much they "confessed," never were able to attain the level of trouble-free living they often were promised. Rather their lives continued to be fraught with suffering and sorrow. This condition left them in the class of the "faithless," and they began to feel like second-class citizens of the kingdom. "There must be something wrong with me" became a common concern.

I believe that one of the original intents of the faith message was to move people away from negativism, bitterness, and criticism—an excellent goal. But much of that intent seemed to get lost in the message of "perfection living." And soon the lack of reality in this message brought great discouragement. If more emphasis had been placed on the other side of this "spiritual coin," perhaps there would have been fewer casualties. The other side acknowledges that we are in a spiritual war, and, as happens in any battle, soldiers are going to be wounded. That means suffering, sorrow, pain, sacrifice, self-discipline, and a multitude of other struggles will come.

But some of the faith proponents find such a message repugnant. They assert that one must never "confess" the existence of these negatives. It's much like believers who won't speak of Satan because it's not positive to do so. Hence they remain ignorant of his devices and live ineffective lives year after year.

If the faith message is to be realistic and effective, it must incorporate the teaching that troubles will come and sometimes seem to stay, so our greatest victory will be in shunning negativism, bitterness, and criticism—not in claiming these things do not exist.

The whole of the gospel message is one of warfare. "Endure hardship with us like a good soldier of Christ Jesus" (2 Tim. 2:3). It's a message of constant battle until the end of our lives or of this age, whichever comes first. Charles Spurgeon said, "The Lord gets his best soldiers out of the highlands of affliction." D. L. Moody exhorted, "Take courage. It is sweet to talk with God; we walk in the wilderness today and in the promised land tomorrow."

So there are two sides to the valid faith message: one

is of immediate blessing and victory, the other of suffering and sorrow. Since few of us have problems accepting the blessing and victory side, we will take a look at suffering and sorrow.

SUFFERING, MATURING, AND VICTORY

Let's establish some basic principles. First, *when we correctly approach the sufferings and sorrows we encounter in this life, they can lead us to greater victory and a more fruitful ministry.* We will have problems and trouble. They are unavoidable. But Scripture makes it clear that God wants to face every problem with us: "If God is for us, then who can be against us" (Rom. 8:31); "Cast all your anxiety on him" (1 Pet. 5:7); "Trust in the Lord with all your heart" (Prov. 3:5); "Do not worry about your life" (Matt. 6:25). These verses all indicate God's provisions to us as his children, as well as his guarantee of help in time of trouble.

If God is willing to fight with us and for us then there is not one battle in life that we need to face with a negative perspective. We can face every situation with the confidence that he will see to it that all will work out for our good (Rom. 8:28).

Second, *suffering and sorrow may come to a Christian from several different sources.* Even committed believers find that at times God allows things to come their way to test the fiber of their makeup and to make them stronger. These tests allow Christians to see their strengths and weaknesses. Many times the revelation of weakness prevents spiritual pride.

Third, *sometimes God corrects and disciplines us in ways that are painful to keep us from making future mistakes.* The writer of Hebrews, quoting Proverbs, says: "My son, do not make light of the Lord's discipline, and do not lose heart when he rebukes you, because the Lord disciplines those he loves, and he punishes everyone he accepts as a son." He then goes on to encourage us to "endure hardship as discipline; God is treating you as sons. For what son is not disciplined by his father? If you are not disciplined (and everyone undergoes discipline), then you are illegitimate children and not true sons" (Heb. 12:5-8).

Fourth, *adversity can come from the enemy of our souls, so we need to learn to recognize the origin of adverse experiences.* God's adversity is meant to direct us in the way of life; the enemy uses adversity to destroy our commitment to our Savior and to the gospel message. Jesus said to Peter, "Simon, Simon, Satan has asked to sift you as wheat" (Luke 22:31). Then, after Peter had gone through that sifting process, he wrote to the Church and said, "Be self-controlled and alert. Your enemy the devil prowls around like a roaring lion looking for someone to devour" (1 Pet. 5:8).

Fifth, *problems can come from our own foolishness.* This is called the "law of sowing and reaping": "For he who sows to his flesh will of the flesh reap corruption; but he who sows to the Spirit will of the Spirit reap everlasting life" (Gal. 6:8, NKJV). Though God is willing to forgive, the errors we make in life often leave scars that are visible for the rest of our lives.

Sixth, *we face problems because our planet is still in the middle of the redemption process.* Every great man or woman who has ever served God faithfully has faced difficulty. Peter, we know, was one such person. From the experience of many trials and experiences he wrote, "Dear friends, do not be surprised at the painful trial you are suffering, as though something strange were happening to you. But rejoice that you participate in the sufferings of Christ, so that you may be overjoyed when his glory is revealed" (1 Pet. 4:12-13). Peter believed that struggle would give us needed strength: "And the God of all grace, who called you to his eternal glory in Christ, after you have suffered a little while, will himself restore you and make you strong, firm and steadfast" (1 Pet. 5:10). Sometimes incredible problems have to take place in people's lives before they will mature and gain a proper perspective.

Paul was acquainted with struggle, but he definitely was not one to let it get him down: "Not only so, but we also rejoice in our sufferings, because we know that suffering produces perseverance; perseverance, character; and character, hope. And hope does not disappoint us, because God has poured out his love into our hearts by the Holy Spirit whom he has given us" (Rom. 5:3-5). "I consider that our present sufferings are not worth comparing with the glory that will be revealed in us" (Rom. 8:18). "[Let] no one . . . be unsettled by these trials. You know quite well that we were destined for them. In fact, when we were with you, we kept telling you that we would be persecuted. And it turned out that way, as you well know. For this reason, when I could stand it no longer, I sent to find out about your faith. I was afraid that in some way the tempter might have tempted you and our efforts might have been useless" (1 Thess. 3:3-4).

Paul encouraged the Corinthians to realize that the glory of eternal life awaited them in the midst of trouble: "For our light affliction, which is but for a moment, is working for us a far more exceeding and eternal weight of glory" (2 Cor. 4:17, NKJV). In this verse the apostle wasn't saying that our afflictions would end in a matter of weeks or months or any brief duration of time. The word *moment* here speaks of our present troubles, which will last throughout our life span (see James 4:14). It refers to the fact that all our lives here on earth will be open to trouble: "Yet man is born to trouble as surely as sparks fly upward" (Job 5:7). Even Jesus said, "In this world you will have trouble" (John 16:33).

David the Psalmist said, "Before I was afflicted I

went astray, but now I obey your word" (Ps. 119:67). He went on to say, "It was good for me to be afflicted so that I might learn your decrees" (Ps. 119:71).

A POSITIVE ATTITUDE TOWARD TROUBLE

There are two Scriptures that equate suffering with overcoming, or where the two terms at least fit in the same context. The first is: "To him who overcomes, I will give the right to sit with me on my throne, just as I overcame and sat down with my Father on his throne" (Rev. 3:21). The second: "If we endure, we will also reign with him. If we disown him, he will also disown us" (2 Tim. 2:12). One indicates that in order to reign we must overcome; the other indicates that in order to reign we must endure suffering, sorrow, and trials (see the King James Version). Evidently, to reign with Christ one needs to be victorious, to overcome. But to overcome we must undergo some trouble in life because we are committed to the war at hand.

This suffering we speak of must never be thought of as asceticism, which is self-inflicted torment. Afflicting oneself physically or mentally in order to appear righteous or to atone for sins is unscriptural. Deliberately seeking to antagonize or stir up situations where we eventually will have to suffer for the sake of suffering is sin. The suffering we speak of is the result of doing battle against the enemy and against the flesh. Taking up our cross daily is like picking up a weapon and going off to war. Sitting back and passively taking whatever the enemy throws our way with the attitude, "I must suffer for Christ," has nothing to do with preparing for battle. There are many Christians who think they are suffering for Christ when in fact they are reveling in self-pity. They love to show what they think are battle scars—an attitude reminiscent to that of the Pharisees who loved to appear righteous for their own glory.

For a positive lesson in overcoming we might look to the Old Testament Hebrew people. Exodus 1:12 says, "But the more they were oppressed, the more they multiplied and spread; so the Egyptians came to dread the Israelites." What a testimony to fortitude and tenacity! What a testimony to endurance! Perhaps nothing catches people's attention as much as a story of one who endured adversity and won, all without self-serving purposes.

No one likes to be in valleys even when they are the consequence of two mountain tops. But it is here in valley experiences that our true inner fiber is determined. Oswald Chambers suggests, "You have had the vision, but you are not there yet by any means. It is when we are in the valley, where we prove whether we will be the choice ones, that most of us turn back. We are not quite prepared for the blows which must come if we are going to be turned into the shape of the vision."[1]

An unknown Confederate soldier adds:

> *I asked God for strength that I might achieve;*
> *I was made weak that I might learn humbly to obey.*
> *I asked God for health that I might do greater things;*
> *I was given infirmity that I might do better things.*
> *I asked for riches that I might be happy;*
> *I was given poverty that I might be wise.*
> *I asked for power that I might have the praise of*
> *men;*
> *I was given weakness that I might feel the need of*
> *God.*
> *I asked for all things that I might enjoy life;*
> *I was given life that I might enjoy all things.*
> *I got nothing that I asked for—*
> *But everything I had hoped for . . .*

> *Almost despite myself my unspoken prayers were answered.*
> *I am among all men most richly blessed.*[2]

SUPREME SUFFERING

Concerning Jesus, the book of Hebrews says, "Although he was a son, he learned obedience from what he suffered" (Heb. 5:8). There is perhaps nothing so startling and moving as the realization of the suffering that God went through at Calvary. The physical torture was horrible, the oppression from the enemy nearly unbearable. And when you add the sin of the whole world to his back, who really can comprehend what he went through? Yet there is more to it than that. It was *God* who was suffering! That is incomprehensible! God was actually in pain while in the process of redeeming his very own creation, a creation that was quick to turn its back on him all in the name of self.

And yet his love was of such magnitude he was willing to offer us hope through his suffering and to say, "Take heart! I have overcome the world" (John 16:33). Now, because he suffered and achieved victory, we also can bear our suffering because we "are from God and have overcome [the spirits], because the one who is in [us] is greater than the one who is in the world" (1 John 4:4).

The message in this chapter, then, is that we must be alert when we undergo suffering and sorrow. We must determine whether our difficulties are something from Satan and his demons; or a means by which God is helping us to stand on "Higher Ground," as an old hymn suggests; or something we ourselves have called forth because of our own desires for the flesh. And we must realize that whatever the source, we are expected to overcome.

So far in our study we have talked about overcoming

the enemy by defensive means. Now let's look at the offensive weapons we have available. And let's consider the fact that God expects us to stand against the powers of darkness and to storm the enemy's gates, which means going from where we are to where he is. Are you ready for the journey?

NOTES

1. Oswald Chambers, *My Utmost for His Highest* (New York: Dodd, Mead and Company, 1935), 278.
2. Tim Hansel, *When I Relax I Feel Guilty* (Elgin, Ill.: David C. Cook, 1979), 89.

NINE

Arming for Offense

In Matthew 17:20, Jesus says this to his disciples concerning the power of authoritative prayer: "I tell you the truth, if you have faith as small as a mustard seed, you can say to this mountain, 'Move from here to there' and it will move. Nothing will be impossible for you."

One of the most unusual illustrations on authoritative prayer comes from seminar teacher Dick Eastman. In his Change the World School of Prayer he tells a story of reformation leader Martin Luther that provides us with an excellent example of speaking to a mountain. In 1540 Luther's close friend, Friedrich Myconius, became extremely ill. Myconius was so convinced he would die that he wrote Luther a farewell letter. After Martin Luther read the letter he sent back an astonishing reply: "I command thee in the Name of God to live because I still have need of thee in the work of reforming the church . . . the Lord will never let me hear that thou art dead, but will permit thee to survive me. For this I am praying, this is my will and may my will be done, because I seek only to glorify the Name of God."

Especially note the closing two sentences of this letter, for history reveals that when Luther wrote this letter Myconius's condition had deteriorated beyond repair. He had even lost his ability to speak. Those around him were certain that in a matter of hours he would be dead. But something happened when Myconius read Luther's powerful letter. Slowly new life began to flow into his body. Not long after, he was completely well. Most amazing—Friedrich Myconius actually outlived Luther by two months.[1]

When Jesus said, "I will build my church and the gates of hell shall not prevail against it" (Matt. 16:18, KJV), he was not proclaiming a "hold the line" or "hang in there, baby" doctrine. He was saying that Satan would soon be on the run and there would be no place for him to hide. Demons would not be able to erect any kind of a gate or fortification that would withstand the forward movement of the Church.

This may sound like a broad statement, but Scripture makes no provision for Christians for anything other than victory—victory over the world, the flesh, and the devil.

Down through the centuries, over and over, mankind has witnessed God's power to smash satanic strongholds. War, famine, disease, and pestilence—all kinds of diabolical situations—have given way to righteousness and peace as believers prayed in the name of Jesus. However, the basic problem has been that believers did not continue to intercede so that there would be continuous peace and health. Their ignorance of the enemy's tactics allowed demon forces to go on playing havoc with life on earth. Too often God's people falter in guarding against the return of Satan's forces.

Since we often do not think to pray until we have problems, most of our praying is done to get us out of trouble. We also are prone to retreat quickly from any disturbance that causes pain. But believers who understand the struggle for control of this earth will fight for victory for themselves as well as for others—and they will stand guard over those victories. Delivered alcoholics will not let down their guard no matter how long it has been since they have had a drink. Reunited spouses will not take for granted the new love God has given them but will protect it vigorously. People who once fell to the evil influence of lust are now careful not to put themselves into compromising situations. These people have learned not only to overcome but also to stand guard over the ground they have won (Gal. 5:1).

We must not forget Christ's powerful words, "I have given you authority to trample on snakes and scorpions and to overcome all the power of the enemy; nothing will harm you" (Luke 10:19). It is only Jesus Christ who can give authority against the enemy. He gives it to enable an effective fight on the warfare plain. It is meant to be used "to demolish strongholds," to "demolish arguments and every pretension that sets itself up against the knowledge of God" (2 Cor. 10:4). This authority is not to be used by the insincere, the carnal, or the unbelieving; it is available only to Christians who desire a close, honest, genuine; and forthright walk with their God and Creator.

Paul told the Corinthians, "For though we live in the world, we do not wage war as the world does. The weapons we fight with are not the weapons of the world . . . they have divine power" (2 Cor. 10:3-4). What are some of these powerful weapons?

THE BLOOD OF THE LAMB

When the Apostle John was "in the Spirit" on the "Lord's Day," one of the things he heard was "a loud voice from heaven say: 'Now have come the salvation and the power and the kingdom of our God, and the

authority of his Christ. For the accuser of our brothers
. . . has been hurled down. They overcame him by the
blood of the Lamb' " (Rev. 12:10-11). It is clear from
this passage that Christians are to take an offensive
stand in dealing with the devil. Many Christians, however, live as if their only hope were to ward off his
blows. This should not be our only approach to the
battle. In the verse from Revelation God shows us some
of the offensive weapons we have at our disposal.

It is in the shed blood of the Lamb, Jesus Christ, that
humanity finds salvation from sin and Satan: "Since
the children have flesh and blood, he too shared in
their humanity so that by his death he might destroy
him who holds the power of death—that is, the devil"
(Heb. 2:14).

Freedom from Bondage to Satan. Jesus was not overcome
by Satan. He had already told the Pharisees, "The reason my Father loves me is that I lay down my life—
only to take it up again. No one takes it from me, but I
lay it down of my own accord. I have authority to lay
it down and authority to take it up again" (John 10:17-
18).

It was the death of Jesus that brought us our freedom. He broke the bonds that held us in slavery to
Satan by his shed blood. We are now free—if we
choose to be.

Freedom from Sin. Christ, the Lamb of God, was the
ultimate sacrifice for our sin. His shed blood is the
cleansing agent that washes us and makes us free from
impurity. "To him who loves us and has freed us from
our sins by his blood, and has made us to be a kingdom
and priests to serve his God and Father—to him be
glory and power for ever and ever! Amen" (Rev. 1:5-6).
For "without the shedding of blood there is no forgive-

ness" (Heb. 9:22). The mighty Judge, God the Father, accepted the life of Jesus as payment instead of sentencing us to death for our sins. The just suffered for the unjust.

But how can a Christian use the blood as a weapon?

First, *by realizing that the blood has already set us free*. Reaffirm over and over in your mind that "it was not with perishable things such as silver or gold that you were redeemed . . . but with the precious blood of Christ, a lamb without blemish or defect" (1 Pet. 1:18-19). In other words, Jesus paid his own blood to redeem us from Satan's bondage and from sin.

Second, when Satan's forces begin to harass, *tell them you know what the blood of Jesus has accomplished and you are not going to be moved by their false accusations*. Some Christians use the phrase "I plead the blood of Jesus" when sensing spiritual attack. This can be effective if they understand that what they are saying is, "I take my stand against you, demon spirit, based upon what the blood of Jesus Christ did at Calvary." As simplistic as it may sound, Satan's soldiers hate to be reminded of the event that secured their downfall. Such open proclamation moves a Christian deeper into authority against these demonic forces. (The word *forces* here implies a military group, not an impersonal energy source. Remember, Satan's agents are personal spirit beings.) Saints need to recognize the redemptive and cleansing work of the blood of Christ in transferring a believer from the kingdom of darkness into the kingdom of light, and we need to remind harassing demons that we know the significance and power of the blood of the Lamb.

THE WORD OF TESTIMONY

Not only is the blood of Jesus a weapon but "the word of their testimony" (Rev. 12:11) is one as well. As previously noted in chapter 6, when God's written Word is spoken against demons it is a powerful *defensive* weapon. But the Word also can be used in our *offensive* thrust against Satan. Christians have become so accustomed to defending themselves against the devil that they don't realize they can actually go into enemy territory to drive the forces of evil back.

But remember, Jesus Christ was an extra-terrestrial. He came to earth from a distant place to invade the forces of darkness. After he did his part—the legal defeat of Satan and the redemption of mankind—he left the field of combat to his followers, his Body—the Church—to "mop up," to finish the task. "I tell you the truth, anyone who has faith in me will do what I have been doing. He will do even greater things than these, because I am going to the Father" (John 14:12). Christ started the process for delivering lost humanity, then invited us to participate in it. Not only are we to "continue to work out [our] salvation with fear and trembling" (Phil. 2:12), but we are to proclaim the salvation message to others as well. We are to become actively involved in the salvation process.

The things Jesus did to point the way to eternal life were based on the Word of God. Any similar work a follower of Christ will do must also be based on the same Word of God. This is why it is important that we know and understand Scripture and learn to use it to defeat the enemy. But to know Scripture is one thing. To use it is quite another.

Peter describes how, from the beginning, the Word of God had power. He wrote: "Long ago by God's word the heavens existed and the earth was formed out of water and with water" (2 Pet. 3:5). God spoke creation into being. Even today the power of the Word of God continues to sustain creation: "The Son is the radiance of God's glory and the exact representation of his being, sustaining all things by his powerful word" (Heb. 1:3).

Jesus cast out demons by the power of his Word: "All the people were amazed and said to each other, 'What is this teaching? With authority and power he gives orders to evil spirits and they come out' " (Luke 4:36). And he told his followers that they could do the same: "He called his twelve disciples to him and gave them authority to drive out evil spirits" (Matt. 10:1).

Notice the Apostle Paul's demonstration of this power: "Finally Paul became so troubled that he turned around and said to the spirit, 'In the name of Jesus Christ I command you to come out of her' " (Acts 16-18). And the evil spirit came out of a girl who was bound with a spirit of divination. Her masters had used her commercially as a fortune teller. But when Paul spoke the Word the demon left.

Peter says that even our salvation is a product of the Word of God: "For you have been born again, not of perishable seed, but of imperishable, through the living and enduring word of God" (1 Pet. 1:23). It is the power of the Word of God that brings new life to decaying humanity. The Holy Spirit, using the Word, penetrates the inner recesses of the human heart, replacing darkness and death with light and life. "The entrance of your words gives light" (Ps. 119:130).

The centurion in Luke 7:7 knew there was power in the words of Jesus and appealed to him to "but say the word and my servant will be healed." There is something powerful about words spoken in truth. And when we understand that we can change things by speaking forth the truth we will discover this power for the glory of God.

Another thing we must understand is that this wellspring of life-giving words—formed and energized by the written Word and by the Holy Spirit—will not be effective if it is tainted with lips that also speak forth criticism, bitterness, or lies. As James 3:1 asks, can a well bring forth both bitter and sweet water at the same time?

Also, we must recognize that our speaking forth does not make us miniature gods. It does not mean that whatever we think needs to be done or re-done is going to happen because we speak it into being in our own power. What it does mean is that there will be times when God leads us and energizes us by his Spirit to use the spoken Word and thereby be powerful instruments for proclaiming light and life. And we will see miracles take place as we use the ministry of speaking forth powerful truth to establish *God's* kingdom.

THE NAME OF JESUS

There is a powerful injunction in Paul's letter to the Colossians: "And whatever you do, whether in word or deed, do it all in the name of the Lord Jesus, giving thanks to God the Father by him" (Col. 3:17). By accepting this admonition we become the extension of his ministry.

The name of Jesus, however, is not some magical force. It is not in the realm of charms, amulets, and talismans. It is a declaration of bestowed authority. When a police officer arrests a person, he can say, "I arrest you in the name of the law." He is saying, in essence, "I arrest you according to the laws of this municipality." There is no magic in his word, but there certainly is authority because the offender recognizes this person to be a representative of the government. And because the person knows the government represented will use force to uphold its laws, it usually takes no more than a word for him to give in.

It is similar when believers use the name of Jesus to

do battle in the spiritual realm. We back up our demands by letting demon forces know that we have been commissioned by Christ as his representatives. Just as a police officer uses a gun to enforce his commission, Christians use prayer. If a demon refuses to remove himself at your request, the next step is to call for reinforcements. Prayer then brings heaven's host. And there is not one demon who can stand before that army. "In the name of Jesus" means, "According to the authority vested in me."

But beware! A police officer does not make up the rules while he drives the streets; rather he carries out predetermined directives. It is the same with us. We need to be ready to go through a kind of "officer's training" with God until we understand his plans and procedures.

The sons of Sceva in Acts 19 did not understand God's power as delegated authority. They saw it as mystical power. When they tried to come against demonic forces they found out quickly that without a commission from God through a personal relationship with Jesus Christ not only did the demons remain, they turned and counterattacked. This little event nearly cost these men their lives.

Simon the sorcerer in Acts 8 was another person who thought the power of God was something magical. He even offered to buy it. But this power cannot be bought; it is a free gift to those who will obey the Lord.

There is power in the name of Jesus for many things. The following are but a few:

Power for healing. "By faith in the name of Jesus, this man whom you see and know was made strong. It is Jesus' name and the faith that comes through him that has given this complete healing to him, as you can all see" (Acts 3:16; see also James 5:14).

Power for salvation. "Salvation is found in no one

else, for there is no other name under heaven given to men by which we must be saved" (Acts 4:12; see also Acts 16:31).

Power for deliverance. "He called his twelve disciples to him and gave them authority to drive out evil spirits" (Matt. 10:1; see also Luke 10:19-20; 2 Cor. 10:3-4).

Power for prayer. "And I will do whatever you ask in my name, so that the Son may bring glory to the Father. You may ask anything in my name, and I will do it" (John 14:13-14; see also John 16:23-24).

Power for sanctification and justification. "But you were washed, you were sanctified, you were justified in the name of the Lord Jesus Christ and by the Spirit of our God" (1 Cor. 6:11; see also Heb. 10:10,14).

PRAISE

During the reign of Jehoshaphat, there came a time when the Moabites, the Ammonites, and soldiers from Mount Seir declared war on the people of Judah (2 Chron. 20). Jehoshaphat was afraid at the news and set out with his people to seek God by prayer and fasting. He was certain Judah would be defenseless against the size of the army he knew was marching his way.

While the people stood before God, the Spirit of the Lord came upon Jahaziel saying, "Do not be afraid or discouraged because of this vast army. For the battle is not yours, but God's" (20:15). Fearful of impending doom, the nation had humbled itself and sought the Lord. When God spoke through Jahaziel it was then up to the people to listen and obey. But the battle strategy was quite unconventional: "After consulting the people, Jehoshaphat appointed men to sing to the Lord and to praise him for the splendor of his holiness as they went out at the head of the army, saying: 'Give thanks to the Lord, for his love endures forever'" (20:21).

Can you imagine a military maneuver in which a choir is to go out in front of the troops? That is exactly what happened! Singers were to march out ahead of the army singing praises to God. It probably wasn't nearly as hilarious to the vocalists as it might have been to everyone else. But it was God's plan and it worked. "As they began to sing and to praise, the Lord set ambushes against the men of Ammon and Moab and Mount Seir who were invading Judah, and they were defeated" (v. 22).

Why such a strange approach to warfare? Israel was about to discover the necessity of winning battles spiritually before approaching them naturally. Just as Paul taught, "For our struggle is not against flesh and blood, but against the rulers, against the authorities, against the powers of this dark world and against the spiritual forces of evil in the heavenly realms" (Eph. 6:12), so the Israelites were to learn the same principle. Behind the scenes, Satan's forces work to motivate natural animosity and hostility. So the marauding armies were influenced by demons.

But how can praising and singing to the Lord work to defeat spiritual enemies? If you remember Satan's five "I wills" (see chapter 1) you will remember that one of them was, "I will sit enthroned on the mount of assembly" (Isaiah 14:13). Satan wanted to be praised. Angels enjoy God's love and express their love to him in praise and adoration. Satan wanted that same kind of attention. Yet for all of his desire to be lauded he has never received one ounce of true praise, and he never will. God is praised because of his love. Satan possesses no love and hence cannot truly be praised. All those who serve the enemy do so out of fear, coercion, and selfish motives.

When God is praised out of men's conscious free will,

Satan and his demons hate it. The enemy won't stay around to see and hear God being praised. When Christians praise God willfully, even in the midst of battle, they rout Satan's demons.[2]

SINGING

Singing is a vehicle for declaring the Word of our testimony and for expressing the voice of our praise, whether in a corporate gathering or privately. For the Christian there are two primary types of singing to consider. First, we sing of our allegiance to God—of his goodness, his greatness, his love, his mercy, and much more. This is singing *about* God. Second, we sing *to* him, praising him personally, which leads to intimate worship. And, once again, because Satan hates praise to God, he flees at its sound. Many will affirm that they sense a definite change in atmosphere when a group of believers switch from singing *about* God to singing *to* him.

When we sing about the Lord, we declare to men and angels where we have placed our allegiance; we declare which side we are on. Such declaration begins to set the stage for spiritual warfare and drives the enemy from our midst. As Satan's warriors begin to flee we are able to sense God's presence better and it becomes easier to love the Lord in song. And again our singing moves from songs about him to songs to him.

You may have been in services where the song leader somewhat chided the audience for their lack of spontaneous singing. Had he understood spiritual warfare he might have been able to discern the reason for this lack of response. He might have recognized that he was worshiping "in the spirit" because he had spent time prior to the service preparing his heart. And now the congregation needed to do the same by singing a few songs *about* the Lord. He also may have recognized that going back and forth between singing praise songs (those about God) and singing worship songs (those directly to him) can be confusing to the human spirit. It is like a train banging its cars back and forth because it can't get up enough power to make a continuous pull. How beautiful a service can be when sufficient praise songs are sung in order to bring the people to a point of worship.

FASTING

Fasting as a form of spiritual power cannot be denied. Ezra (8:21-23), Esther (4:16), David (Ps. 35:13), Daniel (9:3), and others in Scripture sought God in this manner to overcome obstacles. Fasting basically means to abstain from food. It gives the body a rest and allows attention to be placed on prayer.

We do not fast to get God's attention. We do it to facilitate placing all our attention on him. Frequently when people begin to seek the Lord by fasting, the flesh immediately acts up. Their minds wander, their stomachs growl, their eyelids become heavy, and soon they become discouraged and quit. The spirit indeed is willing, but the flesh is weak.

Fasting helps to take hold of the flesh and put it in its proper place, allowing the spirit the control it needs for communing with God. Fasting is the easiest way to find out how much influence the body and soul have over the spirit. The harder it is to fast, the more dominant the body. Most people find that the body has much more of an upper hand than they imagined. The secret is to continue to fast while counting the body dead to sin (Rom. 6:11).

Short fasts as well as partial fasts are perhaps the best way to begin, especially for those who have had a problem with giving up food. Another good fast might be to eat just the essentials. Leave out all junk food.

Daniel lived on a very simple diet of vegetables and water while in training in Babylon and actually appeared healthier than those who ate the king's food.[3]

PRAYER

S. D. Gordon declared, "The greatest thing anyone can do for God or man is pray. It is not the only thing; but it is the chief thing. The great people of the earth today are the people who pray. I do not mean those who talk about prayer; nor those who say they believe in prayer; nor yet those who can explain about prayer; but I mean these people who take time to pray."[4] A quick look at Scripture reveals that God's hand is moved by men and women who pray. Yet prayer is more than just asking God for things. It includes such elements as thanksgiving, meditation, confession, and much more. And the kind of prayer that does real damage to Satan's kingdom is intercessory prayer. When we pray in intercession it is an act of warfare. It is marching into Satan's territory under the blood-stained banner of the Cross claiming that which rightfully belongs to us in Jesus Christ. What the enemy has stolen by deceiving unwary souls we demand back through powerful praying.

OBEDIENCE

Perhaps the best example of the power of obedience is found in Paul's words to the Romans: "Through the obedience of the one man then they will be made righteous" (Rom. 5:19). Obedience is learning to live under the umbrella of God's protective power. In that light it may be more of a defensive weapon rather than an offensive one. Regardless, it is powerful and it works. It makes the resources of heaven readily available and brings heaven's host to our assistance. But Satan will always slander the ways of God in such a manner as to make obedience seem to be a binding, "no fun" way of life. In reality, it offers the best in life, not only in the life to come but in this life as well.

REVERENCE AND RESPECT

Being aware of God's presence and acting in a manner in accordance with mutual respect creates an atmosphere where good communication with him can take place. Reverence and respect indicate that we are paying attention to the details that make for good fellowship. And it is clear from Scripture that such an attitude opens before us all of God's resources. The author of Proverbs wrote: "The reverence and fear of God are basic to all wisdom. Knowing God results in every kind of understanding" (Prov. 9:10, TLB).

It is true that God does not need to be impressed, but it is also true that he shouldn't receive less regard than employers, good friends, or certain dignitaries. Why is it that a certain lackadaisical attitude sometimes invades the church, especially in the areas of speech, dress, and good manners? Why is it that an attitude of "it doesn't really matter what I look like, God knows my heart" becomes predominant? Could it be that men and women do not go to the house of the Lord as much to meet God as they do to soothe their consciences or to meet with friends? Could it be that many of us are really lazy and because of it have become irreverent? Irreverence no doubt offends God, but it also gives demon spirits a clue as to who their next prospective target may be.

Irreverence springs more from an attitude than from an action. But since action often is the expression of attitude, we must be careful to act in ways that would be most pleasing to the Lord.

In these last two chapters we have examined the

weapons we need to employ to become an overcomer. Yet we need to know more because sometimes our enemy uses "undercover" methods to try to defeat us. These methods are what we call the doctrines of the devil. Come with me to the next chapter as we move deeper into our study.

NOTES

1. Dick Eastman, *Change the World School of Prayer Manual* (copyright, Change The World Ministries, P. O. Box 5838, Mission Hills, Calif. 91345), Section C.
2. Two books on praise worthy of the readers' study include Jack Taylor's *Hallelujah Factor* (Broadman Press, 1984) and Dick Eastman's *A Celebration of Praise* (Baker Books, 1984).
3. An excellent book on fasting, complete with suggestions for short and prolonged fasts, is *God's Chosen Fast* by Arthur Wallis (Christian Literature Crusade).
4. Dick Eastman, *No Easy Road* (Grand Rapids: Baker Book House, 1971), 16.

TEN

Overcoming the Devil's Doctrines

Billy Graham, in his excellent book *Angels: God's Secret Agents,* writes about the goals of the enemy:

> Since the fall of Lucifer, that angel of light and son of the morning, there has been no respite in the bitter Battle of the Ages. Night and day Lucifer, the master craftsman of the devices of darkness, labors to thwart God's plan of the ages. We can find inscribed on every page of human history the consequences of the evil brought to fruition by the powers of darkness with the devil in charge. Satan never yields an inch, nor does he ever pause in his opposition to the plan of God to redeem the "cosmos" from his control. He forever tries to discredit the truthfulness of the Word of God; he coaxes men to deny the authority of God; and he persuades the world to wallow in the deluding comforts of sin. Sin is the frightful fact in our world. It writes its ruin in vice and lust, in the convulsions of war, in selfishness and sorrow, and in broken hearts and lost souls. It remains as the tragedy of the universe and the tool of Satan to blunt or destroy the works of God.[1]

Demons, which are real spirit personalities capable of inhabiting the human body, work through the soul to gain entrance into our spirits. The mind is their primary entry point. They seek entrance for many reasons, including causing illnesses (both mental and physical) and binding us; that is, they work to render us incapable of functioning the way God made us to function. They even perform miracles in order to carry out their tasks (2 Thess. 2:9). To accomplish these objectives, they spread carefully devised doctrines that put us at odds with our Creator. For this they have plans, goals, and methods. By establishing their teachings in our thinking, they create a system that opposes God. From the garden in Genesis to the last battle in Revelation, their purpose is to keep us from the truth.

Demons work through deception. Eve was the first to be deceived when she fell for Satan's lies and disobeyed God by eating of the tree of the knowledge of good and evil. Mankind, swollen with pride because of the Fall, now succumbs easily to lying evil spirits. Paul warned Timothy that "in later times some will abandon the faith and follow deceiving spirits and things taught by demons" (1 Tim. 4:1).

There is a kind of Christian Teflon mentality that suggests that if you belong to Christ he simply puts a protective coating on you and presto! You don't have to be concerned about the enemy and you can't be deceived. If that were true, God would never have warned his people to fight (1 Tim. 6:12), to resist (James 4:7), to put on armor (Eph. 6:11), to stand (Eph. 6:13-14), and to not be deceived (Luke 21:8).

That the world itself is deceived is evident from Scripture. In Revelation 12:9, John speaks of "that old serpent, called the devil, and Satan, which deceiveth the whole world" (KJV). But can Christians be deceived? Can they be tricked into believing doctrines of demons? Yes! That is why Paul says that "some will abandon the faith" (1 Tim. 4:1). What is it that will cause them to depart? It is that they will follow deceiving spirits and things taught by demons." Again Billy Graham writes:

> Satan's greatest disguise has always been to appear before men as "an angel of light" (2 Cor. 11:14). The underlying principle of all his tactics is deception. He is exceedingly crafty and clever in the art of camouflage. For Satan's deceptions to be successful, they must be so cunningly devised that his real purpose is concealed. Therefore, he works subtly. . . . His deception began in the Garden of Eden. The woman said, "The serpent deceived me, and I ate" (Gen. 3:13). From that time to this, Satan has been seducing and beguiling. . . .
>
> Satan does not want to build a church and call it "The First Church of Satan." He is far too clever for that. He invades the Sunday school, the youth department, the Christian education program, the pulpit and the seminary classroom.[2]

Because we need to be aware of the subtle little ways in which the enemy works, this chapter is devoted to searching out his doctrines. However, we must be careful not to condemn certain teachers who may from time to time unknowingly espouse some of the doctrines of the enemy. Some teachers are simply deceived. They don't recognize the whisperings of Satan's army of spirits, and so they are deceived into mixing Satan's lies in with spiritual truths. As Christians, we must be prepared and willing to test all spiritual teachers by the Word of God, by their characters, and by their attitudes toward the atonement.

Paul cautions the Corinthians concerning Satan's counterfeiting abilities: "For such men are false apostles, deceitful workmen, masquerading as apostles of Christ. And no wonder, for Satan himself masquerades as an angle of light" (2 Cor. 11:13-14).

To the Galatians, Paul mentioned the possibility of angels delivering a false gospel message: "But even if we or an angel from heaven should preach a gospel other than the one we preached to you, let him be eternally condemned" (Gal. 1:8).

Paul also speaks to the Ephesians to keep them from deception: "Then we will no longer be infants, tossed back and forth by the waves, and blown here and there by every wind of teaching, and by the cunning and craftiness of men in their deceitful scheming" (Eph. 4:14).

Paul furthermore shares the problem with Timothy: "Preach the word; be prepared in season and out of season; correct, rebuke, and encourage—with great patience and careful instruction. For the time will come when men will not put up with sound doctrine. Instead, to suit their own desires, they will gather around them a great number of teachers, to say what their itching ears want to hear. They will turn their ears away from the truth and turn aside to myths" (2 Tim. 4:2-4). Satan's tactics of deception quite often employ the strategy of placing his doctrines directly into the religious community where most people would least expect them.

Unfortunately, false apostles are not always easy to recognize. This is why it is vital that we have discernment from the Holy Spirit. We need to be able to see past what a person is saying and into his spirit. But discernment works best when we have knowledge of the Word.

Jesus gives warning concerning false teachers, and some indicators to watch for: "Watch out for false prophets. They come to you in sheep's clothing, but inwardly they are ferocious wolves. By their fruit you will recognize them. Do people pick grapes from thorn bushes, or figs from thistles? Likewise every good tree bears good fruit but a bad tree bears bad fruit" (Matt. 7:15-17).

Following is a study of some of Satan's doctrines. It is intended to give you information that will help you recognize these doctrines should any of them come your way.

THE DOCTRINE OF "MANY WAYS TO SALVATION"

The young demon-possessed girl who followed Paul and Silas while they were on their way to prayer cried out, "These men are the servants of the Most High God, who are telling you *the* way to be saved" (Acts 16:17, italics added). Walter Martin explains that the article *the* here properly translated in the Greek should really be *a*. The demon in the girl was not affirming that Christ was *the only way* to the Father. Rather it was mocking them by declaring that they were just adding another way. The demon was cunningly trying to deceive those who were listening by telling them that Paul was preaching "a way of salvation," but not "the only way."

For centuries Satan has promoted the doctrine of many saviors. He has done this both by raising up men of his own, men over whom he has exerted direct control, and by promoting influential men toward deification, usually after their deaths. Some of these may have been well-meaning men who were either deceived or shortsighted or both, men who would have no idea that their followers would turn them into gods when they were gone.

Satan's tactic is to take attention away from the one true source of salvation: Jesus Christ. Satan uses the many ways from many different doctrines to cause confusion; for multitudes of people it becomes very difficult to determine which way to turn to find truth, and many give up before they really begin.

THE DOCTRINE OF "YOU ARE GOD"

As we have already mentioned, Isaiah tells of five specific "I wills" Satan had concerning his rebellion. One of them was, "I will be like God." One of his primary tactics today is to try to convince us that the very essence of God lies deep within ourselves. "Don't worry about sin and all the negative things you are experiencing," he tells us, "these things are all surface. Once you get past this unimportant exterior you will find that you are a god." Approaching life from this perspective leaves the sin question intact and so we continue to be Satan's slaves. In fact, those who follow this doctrine usually end up finding that the god they were so intently looking for within turns out to be a demon spirit.

When Satan lied to Eve in the garden, telling her that God did not want them to eat of the tree because doing so would show that they were really gods, he told the perfect lie. It made her feel she was missing something, that God was withholding something special from her. Hence, she, and eventually her husband, disobeyed their Creator and sin entered the human race.

The king of Tyrus whom Ezekiel wrote about was duped into believing he was a god. He made the declaration, "I am a god, I sit in the seat of God." He was so deceived that he actually allowed Satan to enter into him. Ezekiel 28:11-19 starts out as a lamentation on Tyrus but expands to the enemy. God was actually speaking to Satan who indwelled this wicked king.

There is something about being a god that is highly pleasing to the old Adamic nature. King Herod, who killed James the brother of John and put Peter in prison, was caught in this same trap. During one of Herod's political speeches, the people responded by shouting that the king spoke with the voice of a god and not a man. This pleased Herod immensely. Instead of silencing the crowd and directing the praise toward God, he continued to allow the exaltation to be heaped upon himself. Scripture says the angel of the Lord struck him down for his sin so that he died. Josephus writes, "He fell into deepest sorrow . . . and he died after five days of illness."

Satan wants to be a god. He has done everything in his power to appear to be one and promises godhood to anyone who will follow him.

THE DOCTRINE OF "KNOWING THE FUTURE"

Years ago I heard something to the effect that if one were to point to the heavens and tell a man that there are 40 sextillion stars in space or direct his attention to the seashore and tell him it contains 100 zillion grains of sand, he would not question you. But point to a door and tell him the paint is wet and he will carry out his own private investigation by touching it or getting close enough to see for himself. Such is the same with the events to come. For whatever reason, we cannot seem to trust the future to God. We want to find and to know it for ourselves. Satan preys on this lack of faith and displays a variety of "toys," all designed to impregnate the human mind with deception: crystal balls, Ouija boards, tarot cards, horoscopes, and palm readings.

These toys, which really are tools of the enemy, help Satan promote the doctrine that "we can know the future." And these simple "toys" seem harmless—especially to the person who does not understand how Satan can work against the minds to eventually gain complete control of a person's entire being.

People who read horoscopes or have their fortunes told can be tempted to wonder if the predictions might really be true. They may even feel that they had better follow the advice they receive to remain healthy and blessed. Such haunting suggestions lead many into superstition and satanic bondage. Instead of living in the love, respect, and admonition of the Lord, people find themselves living in doubt, suspicion, fear, nervousness, and lack of confidence.

THE DOCTRINE OF "ETERNAL PREDICTION"

As surprising as it may seem, demons actually preach a message about salvation. It is usually preached only to the sinner who has a desire to get out of his evil predicament. It is generally stated in this manner, "Some are destined to be saved, others to be damned. You are one of the damned." Some people fall for this devil's lie when they are faced with the guilt of their past along with what seems to be an inability to "get through" to God. Some try to understand spiritual things with their minds, insisting that salvation be explained to their satisfaction before they make the step of all-out surrender to Christ. But the mind cannot comprehend spiritual matters unless the spirit is enlightened. And the spirit cannot be enlightened unless Christ enters a person's heart. Thus these people are deceived into believing that it is a predestined order from God that they must walk the road to hell.

Intercessory prayer and the Word of God can break this bondage. The Word these people need so desperately is, "And everyone who calls on the name of the Lord will be saved" (Acts 2:21). And, "If anyone hears my voice and opens the door, I will go in" (Rev. 3:20). "Everyone" and "if anyone" speaks to every man, woman, or child alive. Salvation is available to all who will believe in the Lord, repent of their sin, and turn from rebellion. Then they will no longer be in cooperation with enemy forces; instead, they will join ranks with the Captain of their salvation who said, "I would that none should perish" (see 2 Peter 3:9).

THE DOCTRINE OF "REINCARNATION"

Demons know that every human has an inner need to be in fellowship with God, so they do everything possible to counterfeit that relationship. For hundreds of years demons have encouraged men to find a "higher reality" with the spiritual dimension—that higher reality, however, has been the product of demon spirits who imitate God. They teach that since it is difficult to encounter God, we may need many lifetimes and even many life forms to accomplish the task. They also teach that not only will we eventually find God in this manner, but we will eventually become gods ourselves. Hinduism is famous for espousing this doctrine of the devil. The tragedy of such a doctrine is that so many people believe it.

THE DOCTRINE OF "YOU'VE GOT TO CLEAN YOUR LIFE UP FIRST"

The satanic lie that says we must clean up our act before we accept Christ works well with many. We seem to know inherently that goodness is associated with knowing God. Since we are aware that our own personal goodness obviously falls far short of God's standards, we are led to believe that God will not accept us as we are. Righteousness, to this way of thinking, is based on how good we are and not on the goodness of God. We erroneously believe that salvation is based on performing good deeds rather than on allegiance to God. Our only hope, we are then tempted to believe, is that someday we will find within ourselves the power to be good; then we will become Christians.

Those who follow this line of thinking are liable to hear another enemy lie when they are on their death beds: "You lived bent on hell this long, you would have to have some nerve asking to come in at the last moment." Satan wants man to procrastinate when it comes to salvation. He has used his "not now, some other time" influence added to the "you're not good enough yet" lie to deceive many.

Scripture tells us that we are saved by grace through faith and not by works (Eph. 2:8-9). God says that man's goodness, no matter how hard he tries, is not good enough (Isa. 64:6). So God offers Christ's goodness to make up for our lack and then implants within us the power of righteousness, giving us the ability to do the good we could not do as an unbeliever. Paul says it this way to the Corinthians: "Therefore, if anyone is in Christ, he is a new creation; the old has gone, the new has come" (2 Cor. 5:17). We do not have the power to clean up ourselves, but Christ does. "Come now, let us reason together, says the Lord. Though your sins are like scarlet, they shall be as white as snow; though they are red as crimson, they shall be like wool" (Isa. 1:18).

Using the Scriptures with gentle, loving persuasion is well worth the time invested in an unbeliever's life to get him to see that this lie he has listened to really does come from the enemy.

THE DOCTRINE OF "EVERYONE IS A CHILD OF GOD"
According to the world, since God created man we are all his children. In the parable of the tares in Matthew 13:36-43, however, Jesus plainly says that some people are children of the kingdom and some are children of the wicked one.

God's definition of fatherhood and childhood is not

based on "begetting" in the physical sense. It has a spiritual basis. A person who follows after the spirit of the world is a child of Satan. One who is born again in spirit and renewed in the power of Jesus Christ is one who is born into the kingdom of God, where God becomes his Father (Rom. 8:15; Gal. 4:6). Paul says to the Romans that we are slaves to the one we obey (Rom. 6:16). In other words, we are of the household of the one we serve.

Scripture makes it clear that salvation cannot be inherited through natural conception. Neither can it be passed on by environment. Being born in a Christian home no more makes a person a Christian with eternal life than being born in a stable makes one a horse. Salvation comes by choice; each person who is confronted with the gospel makes up his own mind as to whether he will follow God into righteousness through Christ or follow Satan into rebellion (see 1 John 3:10).

THE DOCTRINE OF
"GOD IS TOO GOOD TO SEND ANYONE TO HELL"

If Jesus Christ is truly God, there should be no argument over what he said about hell. If he isn't, we need no further discussion. The words of Jesus, however, are very plain on the subject of eternity. "Not every one who says to me, 'Lord, Lord,' will enter the kingdom of heaven, but only he who does the will of my Father who is in heaven" (Matt. 7:21). "You snakes! You brood of vipers! How will you escape being condemned to hell?" (Matt. 23:33).

"If your hand causes you to sin, cut it off. It is better for you to enter life maimed than with two hands to go into hell, where the fire never goes out" (Mark 9:43).

"The rich man also died and was buried. In hell, where he was in torment, he looked up and saw Abraham far away, with Lazarus by his side. So he called to him, 'Father Abraham, have pity on me and send Lazarus to dip the tip of his finger in water and cool my tongue, because I am in agony in this fire' " (Luke 16:23-24). (See also 1 Tim. 2:4 and 2 Pet. 3:9.)

The question is, "Will men believe God when he says there is a place of eternal torment, a place indescribable for its horrible pain, or will they believe the enemy" (see Luke 16:28)? Satan knows that hell is real. He also knows that originally it wasn't created for mankind, but rather for him and his angels (Matt. 25:41). Now he tries to spite God by taking multitudes of men with him, men who would rather listen to the devil's lies than truth from their Creator (Rom. 1:18-32).

THE DOCTRINE OF "JUST LEAD A GOOD LIFE AND DO THE BEST YOU CAN"

I have met people who would strongly assert that they have done their best in certain circumstances. But I have never met anyone who would affirm that in every area and detail of life he had done his best. Every one of us has to admit that somewhere, some place we have let down, we have failed. If doing the best we can were a criteria for salvation, the next thing we would have to determine is "What is best?" and "If I let down once, does that disqualify me?" We also would have to define the degree and intensity of *best*. "Is my best as good as someone else's?" This approach to justifying the right to eternal life has no standard for measurement—and without a standard there can be no assurance, no way of telling whether or not we have been good enough.

Isaiah the prophet sets the record straight as to the innate goodness of man when he says, "All of us have become like one who is unclean, and all our righteous acts are like filthy rags; we all shrivel up like a leaf, and like the wind our sins sweep us away. No one calls on your name or strives to lay hold of you; for you have hidden your face from us, and made us waste away because of our sins" (Isa. 64:6-7).

This "lead a good life and do the best you can" philosophy is basically a problem of self-righteousness— and it was a problem Jesus was careful to confront. He pointed out that God examines the heart rather than praising self-righteous deeds done to impress other men: "You are the ones who justify yourselves in the eyes of men, but God knows your hearts. What is highly valued among men is detestable in God's sight" (Luke 16:15). (Also see Luke 18:9-14 and Rom. 3:9-18.)

God has plainly established that there is no salvation outside of accepting Jesus Christ as our personal Savior (see Acts 4:12). Neither Muhammad, nor Buddha, nor works of self-righteousness, nor any thing, nor any person other than Jesus Christ can bring about eternal life.

OTHER SATANIC DOCTRINES

To the Christian who has failed repeatedly, the enemy whispers, "You have failed God too many times. He won't take you back." To others who have failed and have a poor understanding of God's grace, he declares, "You have committed the unpardonable sin. There's no hope for you."

To one he makes serving God sound as if it were some type of morbid living: "You will have to give up too much in order to be saved." And to yet another he says, "It's not possible to know you are saved."

To some he says, "Once you are saved you can live any way you want. God's grace makes any life-style possible." Others hear, "The Bible is so complicated you can't understand it, so why bother to read it?" And still others entertain the notion, "You are too weak to live a Christian life."

Some people are moved by the lie, "There are too many religions. How can you know which is right?" Or they are convinced that "all Christians are hypocrites" and "the Bible has been translated so many times it's full of errors."

The list of satanic doctrines goes on and on. But they all remain basically the same, which gives credence to the fact that there is one mind behind all of this diabolical thinking. And there is one purpose for promoting these false doctrines: Satan's desire to deceive people into worshiping him and to keep them from ever knowing Christ.

But there is more to the Evil One's battle strategies. There are diabolical methods used by Satan and those who willingly follow him. Those are the things we will consider next.

AN OVERVIEW OF SATAN'S STRATEGY

Satan Worship. As we have already stated, Satan's ultimate goal is to be worshiped as God is worshiped (Isa. 14:14). Those involved in Satan worship are quite aware of what they are doing. They should not be classified with those who operate in ignorance or are deceived. For the most part, Satan worshipers are fully conscious of their actions, and many of them surpass numbers of Christians in their intensity of devotion.

As the world lies in a great deal of deception, not really knowing who is behind the forces that control it, there is a tendency for a kind of ethereal worship. Some have worshiped the sun and the moon and numbers of other physical objects they felt had a spirit within them that controlled some aspect of their lives. They worshiped in ignorance. But this is not the case with Satan worshipers. They are aware of who controls what and in that awareness they blaspheme heavily the things of Christ, making light of him and the cross upon which he hung. Yes, it is true that many in the world are deceived. But a sizable host of people are not. They have determined who they will follow, they have given themselves to a master, they know what they are doing—they willingly follow Satan.

This may seem of little consequence to us, though we may be saddened that anyone should turn his back on Christ. But I'm afraid there are much greater consequences to the actions of those who worship Satan than most of us would like to believe. If they would just worship the enemy and leave Christians alone, we would not need to be so concerned. But this is not the case. Numbers of them are dead set on destroying everything that belongs to righteousness: marriage, the family, morality, religious freedoms. It is said that some even fast and pray to Satan for his help in accomplishing their desires.

The Occult. The word *occult* means "hidden from sight, obscure; to cover or hide; mysterious." Although it is worship of Satan and demons, it differs somewhat from open Satan worship because many who are involved are not fully aware of what they are doing. Some are so deceived they believe they are serving God. Some covens of witches actually refer to themselves as white witches or good witches. Mysticism, magic, and a desire to know the future occupy a great deal of their interest. There are several basic practices of the occult. You may wish to examine these biblical passages in relation to them:

Witchcraft, sorcery, and wizardry—the practice of dealing with demon spirits. Read Exod. 22:18; Lev. 19:31; 20:6, 27; Deut. 18:10-11; 1 Sam. 15:23; 28:3, 9; 2 Kings 9:22; 21:6; 23:24; 2 Chron. 33:6; Isa. 47:9, 12;

57:33; Jer. 27:9; Dan. 2:2; Mic. 5:12; Nah. 3:4; Mal. 3:5; Acts 8:9-11; 13:6-8; Gal. 5:19-21; Rev. 18:23; 21:8; 22:15.

Soothsaying and divination—the practice of fortune-telling and foretelling. Read Num. 22:7; 23:23; Deut. 18:10-14; 2 Kings 17:17; 1 Sam. 6:2; Isa. 2:6; Jer. 14:14; 27:9; 29:8; Ezek. 12:24; 13:6-7; 21:22-29; 22:28; Dan. 2:27; 4:7; 5:7, 11; Mic. 3:7; 5:12; Zech. 10:2; Acts 16:16.

Magic—accomplishing feats by supernatural demon power. Read Gen. 41:8, 24; Exod. 7:11, 22; 8:7, 18-19; 9:11; Dan. 1:20; 2:2, 10, 27; 4:7, 9; 5:11; Acts 19:19.

Enchantments and charms—the practice of casting spells. Read Exod. 7:11, 22; 8:7, 18; Lev. 19:26; Deut. 18:10-11; 2 Chron. 33:6; 2 Kings 17:17; 21:6; Isa. 19:3; 47:9, 12; Jer. 27:9; Dan. 1:20.

Necromancy—the practice of communicating with the dead. Read Deut. 18:11; Isa. 8:19; 1 Sam. 28:7-25; 1 Chron. 10:13.

Prognostication—the practice of predicting or foretelling the future by means of signs or omens. Read Isa. 47:13.

Astrology and star gazing—divination based on the positions of the stars. Read Isa. 47:13; Jer. 10:2; Dan. 1:20; 2:2, 10; 4:7; 5:7-15.

Cults. A cult, according to Webster's dictionary, is a "religion regarded as unorthodox or spurious." It is a system of worship that teaches doctrines other than the true doctrines of Jesus Christ. Cults usually are begun by individuals who either consider themselves messengers from God or are deified in the minds of their followers. But cults can be recognized by comparing their doctrines with the doctrine of Christ. (See chapter 11 for a discussion on the doctrine of Christ.)

Mormonism, Jehovah's Witnesses, Christian Science, the former Oneida Community, the Father Divine movement, the Moonies, Scientology, the Children of

God, and many others fit the dictionary definition of a cult. (Hinduism, Buddhism, and Islam may not always be thought of as cults mainly because of the tremendous size to which they have grown over the years. Yet they contain all the criteria for being cults.)

There are other groups that we would say are not in the "mainstream" of Christianity but differ somewhat from the cults because they usually hold doctrines fairly close to basic Christianity. However, what you hear them saying publicly often is not what they teach privately. Many are "works-oriented." That is, they believe one has to do certain deeds to be worthy of salvation rather than accept God's grace as a free gift through Jesus Christ.

If you encounter people from unfamiliar "Christian" groups, approach them very carefully. You could be trapped in their "fear-oriented" doctrines before you realize it. Check their teachings carefully against God's Word. Be aware of Scripture verses that they lift out of context. See if they demand an overenthusiastic loyalty to a "leader." Watch for constant criticism of other groups. Do they acknowledge that Christ has come in the flesh? (1 John 4:2). Most of all, saturate your mind with the "doctrine of Christ"—which is the next subject on our agenda.

NOTES

1. Taken from *Angels: God's Secret Agents*, © 1975 by Billy Graham. Reprinted by permission of author.
2. Taken from *Approaching Hoofbeats*, © 1983 by Billy Graham. Reprinted by permission of author.

ELEVEN

Winning with the Doctrine of Christ

Billy Graham has this to say regarding God's provision for us today:

> Angels, whether noticed by men or not, are active in our twentieth-century world too....
>
> It was a tragic night in a Chinese city. Bandits had surrounded the mission compound sheltering hundreds of women and children. On the previous night the missionary, Miss Monsen, had been put to bed with a bad attack of malaria, and now the tempter harassed her with questions: "What will you do when the looters come here? When firing begins on this compound, what about those promises you have been trusting?" In his book, *1,000 New Illustrations* (Zondervan, 1960), Al Bryant records the result. Miss Monsen prayed, "Lord, I have been teaching these young people all these years that thy promises are true, and if they fail now, my mouth shall be forever closed; I must go home."
>
> Throughout the next night she was up, ministering to frightened refugees, encouraging them to pray and to trust God to deliver them. Though fearful things happened all around, the bandits left the mission compound untouched.

In the morning, people from three different neighborhood families asked Miss Monsen, "Who were those four people, three sitting and one standing, quietly watching from the top of your house all night long?" When she told them that no one had been on the housetop, they refused to believe her, saying, "We saw them with our own eyes!" She then told them that God still sent angels to guard his children in their hour of danger.[1]

What a wonderful relief it is to know that both God's angels and the truths of Jesus Christ are here to protect us. In the beginning of this book I talked about God's angels, the ministering spirits sent to protect us. But there is nothing quite so valuable for our protection as the doctrine of Christ.

John in his second epistle writes that "anyone who runs ahead and does not continue in the *teaching of Christ* does not have God; whoever continues in the teaching has both the Father and the Son" (2 John 9, italics added).

What is the teaching of Christ? Is it to be found in arguing the merits of Calvinism vs. Arminianism? Is it discovered in debating the issue of speaking in tongues vs. not speaking in tongues? Is it to be found in discussions on how believers dress or about the particular Bible translation they read?

We need only look briefly into the realm of the doctrine of the devil to discover that Satan is interested only in attacking matters that are directly related to the foundational issue concerning redemption: that *only the blood of Jesus Christ cleanses from all sin.* Satan wants us to get so caught up in the less essential matters that we miss what is more important. He delights in stirring debate over inconsequential issues to promote bitterness, strife, and seditions in the body of Christ. Magnifying trivial disputes puts Christianity in a bad light before the world and succeeds in keeping Christians confused over truly important matters. Satan dearly loves to destroy Christian witness by getting Christians riled at one another.[2]

In this chapter we will identify those elements within the doctrine of Christ that are vital to eternal life. This is not to say that these are the only elements of theology that we should study, but they do comprise the core or foundation of biblical Christianity. Certainly a great deal more attention should be given to them than to the side issues. It is from these essentials that multitudes of believers from thousands of different backgrounds, in millions of different places, become "alive" and "alike" in Christ.

You may think as you read these elements of the doctrine of Christ, *Oh, I already know them.* But do you know their implications for defeating Satan, for becoming an overcomer, and for delivering us from sin? Do you know why and how Satan works so desperately to destroy the doctrine of Christ? Do you know that the cults and the occult not only preach their own private doctrines, but that they preach them in such a way as to destroy the foundational elements of Christ—to take away all significance of Christ's shed blood? Indeed, Satan hates the fundamentals of Christianity because they are what will bring him his final defeat.

Following is a brief summary of most of the important elements that relate to the doctrine of Christ.

JESUS CHRIST: SON OF GOD AND GOD THE SON

The Trinity of God is confusing to most of us because we try to understand with our minds things that can only be understood in the spirit. We can understand Jesus as the human part of God, but can we understand that Jesus is also God the Son? The mind labors to understand the Creator; the spirit attuned to him rests in quiet intuitive knowledge.

Paul told Timothy that Jesus was a man: "For there is one God and one mediator between God and men, the *man* Christ Jesus" (1 Tim. 2:5, italics added). "Beyond all question, the mystery of godliness is great: he appeared in a *body*, was vindicated by the Spirit, was seen by angels, was preached among the nations, was believed on in the world, was taken up in glory" (1 Tim. 3:16, italics added). Paul made a similar claim in his letter to the Philippians: "Who, being in the form of God, did not consider equality with God something to be grasped, but made himself nothing, taking the very nature of a servant, being made in *human* likeness" (Phil. 2:6-7, italics added). These verses clearly show that Jesus is the human part, the Son of God. But there is more.

The Bible also teaches that Jesus is God: "In the beginning was the Word [Jesus], and the Word was with God, and the Word was God. He was with God in the beginning. Through him all things were made; without him nothing was made that had been made" (John 1:1-3). "He is the image of the invisible God, the firstborn over all creation. For by him all things were created: things in heaven and on earth, visible and invisible, whether thrones or powers or rulers or authorities; all things were created by him and for him. He is before all things, and in him all things hold together" (Col. 1:15-17; also see Heb. 1:2).

Genesis 1:1 tells us that "in the beginning God created the heavens and the earth." If God created the heavens and the earth, and "by him (Jesus) all things were created," then Jesus must be God. That is the only logical conclusion. And we aren't called on to understand it, but we are expected to believe it.

In Luke 4:8 we read, "Jesus answered, 'It is written: "Worship the Lord your God and serve him only." ' " But in Hebrews 1:6 we read: "And again, when God brings his firstborn into the world, he says, 'Let all God's angels worship him.' " If God is the only one who is to be worshiped, and all the angels of God are commanded to worship the firstborn (Jesus), the only conclusion again is that Jesus must be God.

The religious leaders in Jesus' day looked for ways to kill him. They were upset because he continually broke their man-made Sabbath laws. But the real reason they wanted to put him to death was that he kept referring to himself as God: "For this reason the Jews tried all the harder to kill him; not only was he breaking the Sabbath, but he was even calling God his own Father, making himself equal with God" (John 5:18).

Also, in John 5, Jesus claims equality with God in works (v. 19), resurrection power (v. 21), judgment (v. 22), honor (v. 23), giving of eternal life (vv. 24-25), and eternal existence (v. 26).

Then, in John 8:58, he openly declares that he is God: "I tell you the truth . . . before Abraham was born, I am!" The name "I am" is one of the eternal names of God (see Exod. 3:14), and the Jewish religious leaders knew this very well. That Jesus would call himself God so angered them that they "picked up stones to stone him" (v. 59).

Recognizing that Jesus is the Son of God and also God the Son is a very critical element in the doctrine of Christ. It is one we must believe if we are to claim the name of Christian.

THE VIRGIN BIRTH

Jesus Christ was conceived by the Holy Spirit in the womb of a virgin. It is important that we understand and accept the fact that Jesus did not have a natural earthly father. If we fail to do so we will not understand the power of his sinless life. In chapter 2 we determined that the only way Jesus could escape enslavement to Satan would be to be born sinless. But to be sinless, he would have to be born in a way other than through the natural union between a man and a woman. God's plan was to bring his Son into the world through a virgin. "The virgin will be with child and will give birth to a son, and they will call him Immanuel—which means, 'God with us' " (Matt. 1:23).

Luke records that Mary was a virgin in the fullest sense of the word. She responded to the angel's announcement with surprise: " 'How will this be,' Mary asked the angel, 'since I am a virgin?' " (Luke 1:34). Seven hundred years prior to the actual event, Isaiah prophesied, "The virgin will be with child and will give birth to a son, and will call him Immanuel" (Isa. 7:14).

The Holy Spirit literally planted the seed of God in Mary's womb. The child that was born came to be known as the God-Man, for he was both completely God and completely Man.

In Genesis, God promised that Satan's undoing would come from the offspring of a woman: "And I will put enmity between you and the woman, and between your offspring and hers; he will crush your head, and you will strike his heel" (Gen. 3:15).

Belief in the virgin birth of Jesus Christ is the only way to accept the fact that he was born sinless. Not only was he born sinless, he also lived a sinless life, "Therefore, just as sin entered the world through one man [Adam], and death through sin, . . . through the *obedience* of the one man [Jesus] the many will be made righteous" (Rom. 5:12,19, italics added).

CHRIST'S DEATH RESCUES MAN FROM SIN

As long as we believe the humanistic philosophy that claims we have no sin, we are not in a position to receive eternal life. Blinded by the god of this age, many are not even aware that they are enslaved to sin. But most people eventually experience an inner torment, an emptiness or incompleteness because of their separation from God. Pascal, the seventeenth-century philosopher, physicist, and mathematician, described it as "a God-shaped vacuum that only God can fill." These people try desperately to find satisfaction and fulfillment in life, only to be driven to greater despair. Paul spoke of being a prisoner of the law of sin (Rom. 7:23). This was his condition before Christ entered his life.

But Christ came to die so that he could deliver us from the penalty, power, and presence of sin. These three important deliverances took place at the Cross where Jesus shed his blood. Let's look at them more closely.

First, *he came to deliver us from sin's penalty, assuring us of eternal life.* God's Word firmly declares that we will spend life beyond the grave in one of two places—heaven or hell. Sin separates and banishes us from the presence of God. This condition can be reversed only if we turn to God through Christ before it is too late (Acts. 4:12). God does not want even one person to go to hell. In fact, as has been stated, hell was not created for man—it was created for Satan and his angels (Matt. 25:41).

When we say that the blood of Jesus cleanses us from the penalty of sin, we mean that it also delivers us from the guilt of sin. We are not speaking about emotional guilt but rather the fact of guilt. If we err, it makes no difference how we feel. The fact is that we are guilty. As humans we are already judged as guilty because of sin. We are in error and must pay a penalty. But Christ steps in and says, "I'll pay it for you," and so he delivers us. He sets us free from the penalty and guilt of sin. Here, then, is the true essence of Christianity, that Christ shed his blood on the Cross to cleanse us from all sin.

Second, *Jesus came to free us from sin's power*. The old Adamic nature must be taken care of or it will continue to drive and control us against our will. When we accept the gift of salvation through Christ, things start to change. We take on new life. Evil ways begin to disappear. This happens because Christ, by his Spirit, takes up residence in our human spirits. When Christ enters, the first thing he removes is the old nature with its power to force us to sin: "For we know that our old self was crucified with him so that the body of sin might be rendered powerless, that we should no longer be slaves to sin" (Rom. 6:6).

Third, *Christ came to set us free from sin's presence*. His redemptive work in this area deals with the flesh. By letting the spirit take control, the body does not need to be a channel for sin: "And they that are Christ's have crucified the flesh with the affections and lusts" (Gal. 5:24, KJV). This power for crucifying the flesh comes only as we live by the Spirit: "Walk in the Spirit and ye shall not fulfill the lust of the flesh" (Gal. 5:16, KJV).

CHRIST CONQUERED
DEATH, HELL, AND THE GRAVE

The disciples of Jesus deeply mourned his death. The activities of the final week of his life had brought much confusion to his followers. They were convinced he was the Messiah and thought he had come to establish his earthly kingdom among the nations. They were not aware that with this first coming Jesus was establishing his inner kingdom, a kingdom in the hearts of men. Then, suddenly, he was dead. Their hope was shattered. Jesus had died like a common criminal, crucified between two thieves. It was evident that he was truly dead; a Roman soldier's spear thrust into his side had brought forth the witness of death— blood and water. Finally, when they placed Jesus in the tomb and rolled a large stone over its mouth, there came a silent resignation: "It's final; he's gone."

Triumph over Death. Then, three days later, the disciples heard reports that he was alive. They were generally skeptical since rising from the dead was not a common occurrence. And they could not remember any prophecy from the Lord that he would rise in three days, even though he had said he would (John 2:19).

One day, when the eleven disciples were all together in a house, Jesus appeared in their midst. Even Thomas, who had refused to believe unless he could actually touch him, was convinced. It was Jesus. He clearly was alive!

Many years later on the Isle of Patmos, John beheld him and heard him say, "I am the Living One; I was dead and behold I am alive for ever and ever" (Rev. 1:18). He had succeeded. He had conquered death, and not only death but the devil as well so "that by his death he might destroy him who holds the power of death—that is, the devil" (Heb. 2:14).

Since he has conquered death and Satan, we as believers are assured of victory over the second (spiritual) death: "Because through Christ Jesus the law of the Spirit of life set me free from the law of sin and death" (Rom. 8:2). We will not be part of the second death (Rev. 2:11; 20:6, 14; 21:8) for we have "crossed over from death to life" (John 5:24).

Physical death, however, still has a hold on all of mankind: "Man is destined to die once, and after that to face judgment" (Heb. 9:27). But a day is coming when even this "death" shall be no more. "The last enemy to be destroyed is death" (1 Cor. 15:26). "He will wipe every tear from their eyes. There will be no more death" (Rev. 21:4).

Triumph over Hell. Not only did Jesus conquer death, he also shut the door to hell for anyone who would follow him to safety. The place of eternal punishment is real. In the Old Testament the Hebrews called it Sheol (wrongly called *grave* in KJV); in the New Testament it is *hell* or *hades.*

The rich man who knew Lazarus found its torment unbearable. He begged for a drop of water, then he desired to warn his brothers that they might escape its agony (see Luke 16:19-31).

Hades is the place of torment for departed wicked spirits of men where they are kept until the resurrection of the dead (Rev. 20:11-15). Hades was also the place where the righteous dead were kept until the resurrection of Christ. It was a paradise or place of comfort until Christ rescued them and took them with him when he ascended into heaven (Eph. 4:8-10).

Triumph over the Grave. Jesus also conquered the grave. The grave is not *Sheol* or *hades,* which is the word describing where the departed soul and spirit goes. The grave—*qibrah* (Hebrew) or *mnemeion* (Greek)— is the place where the body is placed until the final resurrection. The word for hell and the word for grave are not the same and they are not interchangeable.

When Jesus rose from the dead he came forth not only in spirit but also in body: "Look at my hands and my feet. It is I myself! Touch me and see; a ghost does not have flesh and bones, as you see I have" (Luke 24:39).

His body did not see corruption as all other bodies do. Rather it was raised from the dead as an eternal, immortal flesh-and-bone body (Luke 24:37-43).

King David had prophesied: "You will not abandon

me to the grave, nor will you let your Holy One see decay" (Ps. 16:10; Acts. 2:27, 31). Christ was "the first-fruits of those who have fallen asleep" (1 Cor. 15:20), for because of him we will also be raised from the dead at the proper time. Our bodies will not be left in the grave, but will come forth incorruptible—that is, immortal. "Listen, I tell you a mystery: we will not all sleep, but we will all be changed—in a flash, in the twinkling of an eye, at the last trumpet. For the trumpet will sound, the dead will be raised imperishable, and we will be changed. For the perishable must clothe itself with the imperishable, and the mortal with immortality. When the perishable has been clothed with the imperishable, and the mortal with immortality, then the saying that is written will come true: 'Death has been swallowed up in victory.' 'Where, O death, is your victory? Where, O death, is your sting?' " (1 Cor. 15:51-55).

RESURRECTION, ASCENSION, AND INTERCESSION

The resurrection of Christ is another aspect of the doctrine of Christ which we must believe. And after his resurrection, Christ ascended into heaven, where he is now seated at the right hand of God and interceding for his people. Jesus left this earth as miraculously as he came to it. He simply ascended. Before the eyes of many witnesses, gravity seemed to release its hold and he began to rise: "He was taken up before their very eyes, and a cloud hid him from their sight" (Acts 1:9). Mark recorded: "After the Lord Jesus had spoken to them, he was taken up into heaven and he sat at the right hand of God" (Mark 16:19).

Scripture further certifies that this event was unique. Others have been taken up (Enoch and Elijah) but never, as in this case, of their own accord. "No one has ever gone into heaven except the one who came from heaven—the Son of Man" (John 3:13; also see Heb. 7:25).

CHRIST IS COMING AGAIN

Jesus is coming back to earth again. Scripture makes this clear. He said plainly that he would come again. There are many aspects of his second coming—rapture, tribulation, battle of Armageddon, etc.—but for now suffice it to say that he *is* coming again: "In my Father's house are many rooms; if it were not so, I would have told you. I am going there to prepare a place for you. And if I go and prepare a place for you, I will come back and take you to be with me that you also may be where I am" (John 14:2-3).

When Jesus returns to earth he will set up the final world kingdom, a kingdom under the Messiah: "The God of heaven will set up a kingdom that will never be destroyed, nor will it be left to another people. It will crush all those kingdoms and bring them to an end, but it will itself endure forever. This is the meaning of the vision of the rock cut out of a mountain, but not by human hands—a rock that broke the iron, the bronze, the clay, the silver and the gold to pieces. The great God has shown the king what will take place in the future" (Dan. 2:44-45).

Daniel further records that it will be an everlasting kingdom ruled by the saints of God: "In my vision at night I looked, and there before me was one like a son of man, coming with the clouds of heaven. He approached the Ancient of Days and was led into his presence. He was given authority, glory and sovereign power; all peoples, nations and men of every language worshiped him. His dominion is an everlasting dominion that will not pass away, and his kingdom is one that will never be destroyed. . . . But the saints of the Most High will receive the kingdom and will possess it forever—yes, for ever and ever. . . . Then the sovereignty, power and greatness of the kingdoms under the whole heaven will be handed over to the saints, the people of the Most High. His kingdom will be an everlasting kingdom, and all rulers will worship and obey him" (Dan. 7:13-14, 18, 27).

Zechariah also prophesied this event: "On that day there will be no light, no cold or frost. It will be a unique day, without daytime or nighttime—a day known to the Lord. When evening comes, there will be light. . . . The Lord will be king over the whole earth. On that day there will be one Lord, and his name the only name" (Zech. 14:6-7, 9).

Jesus spoke of his second coming in this way: "Immediately after the distress of those days, the sun will be darkened, and the moon will not give its light; the stars will fall from the sky, and the heavenly bodies will be shaken" (Matt. 24:29-30).

Paul told the Thessalonians: "May he strengthen your hearts so that you will be blameless and holy in the presence of our God and Father when our Lord Jesus comes with all his holy ones. . . . Brothers, we do not want you to be ignorant about those who fall asleep, or to grieve like the rest of men, who have no hope. We believe that Jesus died and rose again and so we believe that God will bring with Jesus those who have fallen asleep in him" (1 Thess. 3:13; 4:13-14).

Finally, the Apostle John, describing his Patmos vision says, "Look, he is coming with the clouds, and every eye will see him, even those who pierced him; and all the peoples of the earth will mourn because of him. So shall it be! Amen" (Rev. 1:7).

THE TRUE SOURCE OF SALVATION

Another important Christian doctrine is that we do not earn salvation by any action on our part; Christ provides salvation by grace through faith. Because we are by nature proud and arrogant, "grace" is a difficult concept to understand and accept. Indeed, pride is an enemy that keeps many from entering into full freedom in Jesus.

For example, pride keeps us from freely receiving gifts without trying to give something in return. We experience this when we receive an undeserved or unwarranted gift; we tend to feel the urge to try to compensate or return the favor. This is probably because of an inner desire to make things "even"—to not owe anyone anything. We frequently reflect this attitude in special gift-giving events. Some people will open a birthday or Christmas present and say, "You shouldn't have," and then feel obligated to give a commensurate gift to the giver at a later date.

Eternal life is also difficult to receive as a free gift. Yet this undeserved gift of love is given by God without obligation. No matter how sinful we are or what our personal abilities (or lack of them) may be, grace is available to everyone who is willing to receive it.

Many works-oriented religions have been formed because the founders could not or would not understand God's unconditional love. They believe that salvation must come about by observing laws or commandments or rituals. Then, such works-oriented religionists begin to display an attitude that, because of their own efforts and devotion, they are the only true "children of God." They do not see that salvation is based on allegiance and not on performance. Make no mistake, when Christ is at work within there will be excellent performance, but it will be a performance that comes as a result of salvation, not one that is necessary for it.

God wants to reach past all our self-effort and pride with his love, but our flesh resents such absolute and sovereign love. It says, "There must be a catch. Some place down the road I'll have to pay." Because the flesh is so void of love itself, it can't seem to comprehend love in someone else.

We could never be good enough or charitable enough, or even sacrificial and pure enough, to earn our own salvation. And so we must learn that salvation comes "not by works, so that no one can boast" (Eph. 2:9). "Therefore, since we have been justified through faith, we have peace with God through our Lord Jesus Christ, through whom we have gained access by faith into this grace in which we now stand. And we rejoice in the hope of the glory of God" (Rom. 5:1-2).

Another reason it is hard for some people to receive the gift of grace is fear of failure. When we try in and of ourselves to be worthy of God's love we find that we still fail. Then the feelings of unworthiness and guilt that follow failure further prevent God's work of grace in our lives. But if we understand that, because of sin and rebellion, we are unworthy of fraternizing with God—that we always have been and always will be in that state—then the dimension of God's love is easier to comprehend. "Since I'm this way and can't do anything about it, but God says that he cares and wants to help and that he loves me, I guess that's worth listening to." It is at this point that God begins to change us into that which is pleasing to him.

In Watchman Nee's book *Sit, Walk, Stand,* Nee points out the necessity of sitting with the Lord in heavenly places long enough to understand our position and power in Christ. Then and only then are we able to "walk with Christ" and to "stand to fight" against the enemy.

These are just a few of the fundamentals of our Christian faith. In a day in which men's minds are greatly confused and error is rampant, it is important that we do not waver by straying from the important matters concerning our salvation.

Now, let's look at this whole matter of spiritual warfare from a most vital perspective: prayer.

NOTES

1. Taken from *Angels: God's Secret Agents*, © 1975 by Billy Graham. Reprinted by permission of author.
2. A fine book dealing specifically with the subject of unity in the body of Christ and how that unity can be destroyed by nonessentials to salvation is Paul Billheimer's powerful work, *Love Covers* (Christian Literature Crusade).

TWELVE

Contacting the Supreme Commander

The basic premise of this book is simply that there is an unseen war being waged in the heavenlies. And we have offered many ways to prepare to meet the enemy. But no matter what we do to prepare, no matter how aware we are of the enemy's whereabouts and tactics, we still will lose the war if we fail to fight each battle in prayer. Prayer, indeed, is the way for us to communicate with the command post. It is our method of talking with the Captain (Heb. 2:10).

Unfortunately, the average believer either doesn't understand effective prayer or doesn't realize how vital it is to pray. Most believers regard prayer simply as a way of getting things they either need or want. Although we are encouraged in Scripture to bring our petitions to God, if that is our only reason for praying we will never experience, as the hymn writer says, "the soul's sincere desire. . . . the motion of a hidden fire that trembles in the breast."[1]

If we think of prayer as only asking God for things, we will never realize the beauty of seeking him for who he is and the blessedness of just getting to know him. It is when we touch him in the quietness of time spent alone with him that the necessary faith for miraculous answers to our prayers is granted. But the reason for being there alone with him must never be only to obtain answers. We must approach his presence because of the desire for him and him alone.

S. D. Gordon said, "The greatest thing anyone can do for God and man is pray. It is not the only thing; but it is the chief thing." That's it! It's the most important thing in the life of a believer! But it isn't something we conjure up ourselves. It is something that God has to help us with.

Charles Spurgeon declared, "Prayer itself is an art which only the Holy Ghost can teach us. Pray for prayer—pray till you can pray." And so the Holy Spirit must be involved directly in our praying in order for us to become effective. "But you, dear friends, build yourselves up in your most holy faith and pray in the Holy Spirit" (Jude 20). "In the same way, the Spirit helps us in our weakness. We do not know what we ought to pray, but the Spirit himself intercedes for us with groans that words cannot express" (Rom. 8:26). "And pray in the Spirit on all occasions with all kinds of prayers and requests. With this in mind, be alert and always keep on praying for all the saints" (Eph. 6:18).

E. M. Bounds writing on prayer cautioned, "Prayer is not a little habit pinned on to us while we were tied to our mother's apron strings; neither is it a little decent quarter of a minute's grace said over an hour's dinner, but it is a most serious work of our most serious years."

Obviously prayer is more than just a child's bedtime repetition. And it's more than what a friend of mine jokingly said he prayed in college: "Now I lay me down to rest, tomorrow I've got another test. If I should die before I wake, that's one less test I'll have to take." Indeed, prayer is much, much more. Prayer is a difficult, taxing, spiritual work. And it's not something that comes easily to us because our human nature does not like to take on difficult things. We are much happier at the prospect of coasting into blessings without facing any storms. But because we have to set pride and self aside when we pray, it is work that humbles us. Through prayer we see our spiritual weaknesses and lacks. Often it seems as though it would be easier just to forget about praying than to handle what prayer brings into our lives. But a lack of prayer will only make us weaker; without prayer we end up building a false sense of spiritual security and rightness. So prayer is something we cannot afford to ignore.

Martin Luther said: "As it is the business of tailors to make clothes and cobblers to mend shoes, so it is the business of Christians to pray." And it has been said that to be a Christian without praying is no more possible than to be alive without breathing. As Charles Spurgeon also preached, "God forbid that our prayer should be a mere leaping out of bed and kneeling down, and saying anything that comes first to mind. On the contrary, may we wait upon the Lord with Holy fear and sacred awe." Truly, we need to give more attention to this holy "gift of power" God has given to every believer who will choose to develop it.

PRAYER—A COMMAND

When prayer is recognized as a time set aside for God, it then becomes a delightful experience rather than a time of drudgery. Our world is veiled to the beauty of God, a beauty which only prayer can reveal. A. W. Tozer writes:

> To most people God is an inference, not a reality. He is a deduction from evidence which they consider adequate, but he remains personally unknown to the individual. "He *must* be," they say, "therefore we believe he

is." Others do not go even so far as this; they know of him only by hearsay. They have never bothered to think the matter out for themselves, but have heard about him from others, and have put belief in him into the back of their minds along with various odds and ends that make up their total creed. To many others, God is but an ideal, another name for goodness, or beauty, or truth; or he is law, or life, or the creative impulse back of the phenomena of existence . . .

Christians, to be sure, go further than this, at least in theory. Their creed requires them to believe in the personality of God, and they have been taught to pray, "Our Father, which art in heaven." Now personality and fatherhood carry with them the idea of the possibility of personal acquaintance. This is admitted, I say, in theory, but for millions of Christians, nevertheless, God is no more real than he is to the non-Christian. They go through life trying to love an ideal and to be loyal to a mere principle . . .

[But] the Bible assumes as a self-evident fact that men can know God with at least the same degree of immediacy as they know any other person or thing that comes within the field of their experience.[2]

Not only is prayer a key that unlocks God's power, it is a key our Lord commands us to use! The Scripture says, "Watch and pray" (Matt. 26:41); "Pray continually" (1 Thess. 5:17); "Men ought always to pray, and not to faint" (Luke 18:1, KJV); "Ask the Lord of the harvest" (Luke 10:2); "After this manner therefore pray ye" (Matt. 6:9, KJV).

When you add to this such Scriptures as, "Pray that you will not fall into temptation" (Luke 22:40), or "Is any one of you in trouble? He should pray" (James 5:13), there certainly can be little argument as to whether or not we should pray. Prayer is essential to the ultimate defeat of sin and of demon spirits.

Because prayer is so vital, the enemy ferociously

attacks our every effort to pray. That coupled with the fact that the flesh is not interested causes us to do very little praying. We find that although we want to pray, our minds wander, we grow weary, we become lazy, the busyness of the day distracts us, sin hinders us, personal problems slow us down, and a dozen "good" things interfere with our daily appointment with Jesus.

The only way we will ever overcome these problems of faithlessness in prayer is to make a fierce "prayer goal" to become a prayer warrior. I use the term "prayer goal" rather than suggest making a "vow" in a biblical sense because that way, if we fail, we simply start over again the next day—without condemnation.

As we develop our daily "prayer goal" we must always keep our focus on Jesus. Christ alone is the greatest example of a prayer warrior. It's amazing that he, being God, felt it a necessity to pray. Think of it! If our Lord saw the need to be faithful in prayer, then how much more do we need to give ourselves to this vital holy act. The Bible says of Jesus: "He went up into the hills by himself to pray" (Matt. 14:23); "And I will ask the Father" (John 14:16); "He withdrew about a stone's throw beyond them, knelt down and prayed" (Luke 22:41); "And being in anguish, he prayed more earnestly" (Luke 22:44).

Even more amazing is the fact that Jesus is still involved in prayer: "He always lives to intercede for [us]" (Heb.7:25); "We have one who speaks to the Father in our defense—Jesus Christ, the Righteous One" (1 John 2:1).

A PLACE TO BEGIN: GETTING TO KNOW GOD

In the first five words of Philippians 3:10, Paul says, "I want to know Christ." Somehow we sense Paul is talking about knowing God far beyond the act of personal salvation. You can almost hear this chief apostle shout with a fervency, "Oh, that I may know him!" The secret to prayer is to *know* God. As Jack Hayford suggests in a sermon he once preached: "If we are going to have God's purpose fulfilled in us, we're going to have to get a proper understanding of God the Father. And for some of us the view is pretty loused up. We will never be able to submit to a total relationship with our Heavenly Father and see the outworking of his purpose in every detail of our lives any more than we really know him and trust him and understand how he really feels toward us."

In Daniel 11:32 we read, "And the people that do know their God shall be strong and do exploits" (KJV). What is it that gives this strength? It's getting to know God. Interestingly the word for "know" used here in Daniel is the same Hebrew word, *yada,* used in Genesis 4:1 where we read, "And Adam knew [yada] Eve his wife; and she conceived" (KJV). Perhaps God has allowed the use of this very intimate word in relationship to him so that we would be much more aware of how really close he wants us to be. But the only way we will ever really get to know God is by learning to spend time alone with him. And it takes time.

Time is necessary for developing good skills and good relationships. You will never get to know someone until you spend time with that person. But it takes effort to make it happen. Notice, it's not *taking* time but *making* time that's important. And not only must we put aside time for a "devotional hour" but, once we establish a commitment and make a regular time for prayer, we have to make time while praying to wait quietly before the Lord so that he can respond to us.

Isaiah 40:31 speaks of renewed strength to those who wait upon the Lord. David also knew the value of waiting for God to respond: "Wait for the Lord; be strong and take heart and wait for the Lord" (Ps.

27:14). The primary root for the word *wait* here means "to bind together," perhaps as a rope is bound together by twisting. In another psalm David says: "Be still before the Lord and wait patiently for him" (Ps. 37:7); "Wait for the Lord and keep his way" (Ps. 37:34).

As we spend time alone with God, we will eventually learn that prayer is much more than just asking God for things and then getting answers. We will learn that the true meaning of prayer is to come into the presence of God himself.

ELEMENTS OF PRAYER

We have established that prayer is vital to our knowing God, and our knowing God is vital to our overcoming, but where do we begin in our quest to develop effective prayer? The following elements of prayer should help you begin. Don't be surprised if God helps you expand these in a multitude of ways as you learn to pray daily.

Worship the Lord. Here's what to do:

Praise the Lord! Read 2 Samuel 22:4; 1 Chronicles 16:25; 2 Chronicles 20:20-22; 29:2; Psalms 9:1-2; 63:3-4; 86:12; 113:1-3; 134:2. Take a few moments to audibly praise God. You probably will find that in your quiet time you may not *feel* like praising. But since God is worthy regardless of feelings, the proper thing to do is praise him anyway. Do it as an act of your will. Put aside any stubbornness or inner hesitation and simply begin. You might start by saying, "Father, I worship and praise you because you are worthy. Blessed be your holy name. Receive glory and honor and power and praise, for you and you alone are God. There is no one mightier than you. There is no one above you. You deserve all of my love, devotion, and attention. I praise your glorious name." This may seem somewhat formal but at least it is a start.

You may want to conclude your praise by sharing various feelings from your heart, such as: "Father, I want to learn to love you more. I want my praise to you to come from my heart. May I learn to know you better and to please you in every way." As you share with him in such a manner you will begin to sense his love. Learn to respond to his love by, in turn, offering up more praise. The very essence and root of praise is simply saying, in response to his love, "I love you too."

Sing to the Lord. Read Psalms 9:11; 27:6; 47:6-7; Ephesians 5:19. Singing as a demonstration of praise seems to allow better and deeper expressions of adoration to come from the heart. Done without instruments and in private it may not seem as spontaneous as you would like. However, the use of good Christian tapes and records can be a real blessing in helping to express yourself in song as you pray.

Thank the Lord. Read Psalms 18:49; 26:7; Philippians 4:6. In a seminar I was conducting on the subject of prayer, a young lady came to me and said that she had been going over her past and thanking God for all the good things that had happened to her. Almost immediately I felt convicted. I really don't think I'm much of a negative person. But, like so many of us I am capable of complaining about the bad things that have transpired in the past. As a result of what she said, I made a commitment that I would never again look back and complain. Rather, if I were to look back, it would be with the idea of thanking God for all the good things that he has done.

Wait upon the Lord. Here's what to do:

Meditate. Read Joshua 1:8; Psalms 19:14; 119:15. Meditation can be very dangerous if you fail to understand God's way to use this unique form of prayer.

Godly meditation is active thinking, not passively blanking out the mind so that it becomes like a fresh sheet of blank paper on which anything new can be written. Since the mind is the battlefield, Satan would dearly love to write some of his thoughts on it. Remember, God wants to speak to your spirit so that your spirit can speak to your mind. Satan works in reverse, speaking to the mind trying to get his message to the spirit. When you meditate, you want to think about a particular passage of Scripture and how it relates to you. Or, you want to think about some spiritual theme and then find Scriptures that pertain to it. It can be a real blessing to sit in God's presence and ponder particular thoughts that concern your relationship with him.

Listen. Read Ecclesiastes 5:2. Again, since the mind is the battlefield, you must be very careful that what you hear is really coming from God. Many Christians have been sorely affected by messages that were supposedly from God but were not. Learning to listen takes time and comes about by experience. And the more time spent examining his Word while in prayer, the easier it is to hear his voice.

Read the Word. Read Psalm 119:130; 2 Timothy 2:15. As suggested above, the "Word" is important in prayer. Frankly, it would not be unreasonable to spend half your prayer time reading the Word. What God has to say through his Word is just as important as what you have to say to him. Any meaningful conversation ought to be two-way.

Speak to the Lord. Here's what to do:

Confess. Read Isaiah 1:18; 1 John 1:9. Confession is basically an apology. It is learning to say "I'm sorry, I was wrong!" At times your praying will need to start with this element so your heart is fully prepared for a meaningful time of worship.

235

Ask for things. Read Matthew 7:7; 1 John 5:15. God does not teach that he will give you *only* the basic needs in life. But as a Father, God wants to give you every enjoyable and good thing as long as it won't hurt you or interfere with your participation in the war.

I remember fishing with my son along the edge of a lake and watching those in a boat doing much better than we were doing from shore. Rob and I decided to pray that God would provide us with a boat. We weren't looking for an aircraft carrier. Jokingly, I've said that a thirty-seven-foot cabin cruiser would have done just fine. But really, all we wanted was a ten- to twelve-foot boat that would get us safely away from the shore. We were pleased when, as a gift, a group of people provided the money for the very purpose of buying that boat. Jesus invited us to ask for "good gifts" (Matt. 7:11; 21:22).

Often our basic problem, even as children of the King, is that we are very materialistically oriented. That motivation keeps us from recognizing the real priorities of life. Thus we find ourselves asking amiss (James 4:3).

Another very real problem that many Christians face is the belief that God wants to make all of the decisions in our lives. It is true he would like to make or help make many more decisions than most of us allow, but only from the standpoint that we need help in determining what is best. I have been surprised to find there are times when God does not mind which direction we chose. As we mature in Jesus, there will be times when we ask God for something and he will say "Yes." Other times he will say "No." Sometimes it will be "Wait." But don't be surprised if he says, "You choose. You do whatever you desire; I will approve your decision because I know you will make it on the basis of my Word and that is what pleases me."

It is sometimes difficult for us to believe that God wants us to be people who can make decisions. We think he just wants to control us for his own personal pleasure or so that we will not make mistakes. With this attitude we tend to believe he will give us just the opposite of what we have desired in prayer. With that mentality we might be tempted to manipulate our prayers. We might begin to think, "Let's see now, I want item A but that means God will probably give me item B. Therefore, I'll pray for item B and maybe that way I'll get item A." Until faith, love, and trust are fully established, we think God is against the things we desire.

Intercede. Read 1 Timothy 2:1. Love is never more fulfilled than when you do something for someone else without the slightest desire for either recognition or compensation. When you go to God on behalf of others, praying for their well-being, you fulfill the law of Christ. To stand before God on behalf of a friend or even an enemy is one of the greatest acts of love that can be done. Even Jesus made "intercession for the transgressors" (see Isa. 53:12).

PRAYERS TO PRAY

You may be asking "How do I pray?" and "What do I say when I talk to God?" The following are specific examples of ways in which to pray. Keep in mind that these suggestions are only guidelines; they are designed to help you begin. And as you pray, remember, it is not worth praying about something until you really *desire* the answer. As Jesus said, "what things soever ye desire, when ye pray, believe that ye receive them, and ye shall have them" (Mark 11:24, KJV). Having the desire (and actually asking) often is the key to effective prayer.

Praying to Overcome Temptation. Temptation is always difficult, especially when we are tempted in areas in which we have frequently failed. Temptation, of course, is not a sin. Yielding to the temptation is what causes sin. Most of us know we should avoid anything or any place where we might be confronted with a compromising situation. But realistically we all face situations of potential difficulty. How should you approach such tests? Be totally honest with the Lord over what you feel is going on inside. He won't be surprised. He knows it already. He will listen and help. Here is an example of what you might pray: "Father, I'm having trouble right now. I'm being pulled in a direction I know is wrong. I need your help to walk away from this without sinning. I want to please you but something in me is pulling me toward doing wrong. I accept your help right now."

When I pray such a prayer I often begin to feel the power to resist. And all I need to do at that moment is exactly that: resist. Often that resistance amounts to simply getting up and walking away. It is a good idea to talk to the Lord beforehand concerning the times you anticipate temptation might come. Remember the words of Jesus: "Watch and pray so that you will not fall into temptation. The spirit is willing, but the body is weak" (Matt. 26:41). Talking it over with God ahead of time also helps prevent the temptation from taking us by surprise.

Praying to Change Bad Habits. My grandfather used to tell a story about his problem with smoking. After he received Christ into his life he prayed that God would take the habit away from him. Although his prayer was sincere he had some difficulty with doubt. One day when leaving the house, he realized he might have a need for a cigarette while gone. So he tore one in half and placed a portion in his pocket. In spite of his doubt, God heard his previous prayer, and later when he tried to smoke the cigarette he became so ill he never touched one again.

Here is the key attitude to praying effectively against any habit: *You must really want to overcome.*

So here is a suggested prayer: "Father, I ask your assistance in overcoming a desire for cigarettes [or whatever the habit might be]. Make the smell and taste of them so sickening that I will never want another."

Praying for Healing. We seem most prone to doubt when a physical problem exists. We seldom ask "Can God heal?" Rather, it's usually, "Will he?" Scripture makes it clear that he wants us to be whole. Sickness is not a part of his plan for his children. When Jesus walked the earth he took care of maladies wherever he went.

What then should your attitude be in this area? First, pray for the need with as much faith as you have at that moment. Then continue to seek God until the answer comes. Once when I suffered with a minor physical problem, I found myself saying, "I won't put up with this." I simply refused it and it went away. Now it doesn't always work like this. Growing in grace and faith in overcoming sickness is a process. I wish I could say that anything that comes my way will be met with mountain-moving faith, but I know every situation will have to be worked through as it comes along. And some things will be easier than others.

What then should you pray? Simply, "Lord, heal this illness! Father, help me to see and do the things necessary to bring this healing about. Show me what lessons I am to learn during this difficulty. Help me to be a positive witness to those who are watching me. May you be glorified in every aspect of this problem, including the pain. I do not want to use this affliction to draw attention to myself; therefore, help me to watch my attitude so that it is positive and loving. Help me to guard my inner feelings from bitterness, criticism, and negativism. Father, I am waiting for your miracle." As you conclude your prayer be sure to add praise to your requests, thanking God that he answers prayer, and that he, indeed, is teaching you about his nature and character through this trial.

I recall a particular situation in which I was praying and trying to exercise faith for a physical problem. A minor illness had left me somewhat weakened. As I set about believing for healing, I didn't receive restoration right away and began to doubt. "If God doesn't answer this prayer, then what guarantee do I have that he will answer any other of my requests, especially those that aren't of a physical nature?" God had to jerk me back into reality. Today, I go forward seeking the attitude that whether my faith for the things I want or need works or not, I will continue to seek him.

Praying for Good Relationships. Who hasn't had problems with a relationship—whether it be a spouse, a parent, a child, an employer, or even a friend? But if your prayer focuses only on "change this person or that person" so that you can feel better about or not be hassled by the person, you probably will not experience the blessing of a dynamic answer to your prayer. Your attitude should begin with a desire that your contribution to the relationship will be all that it should be. Indeed, don't be surprised if God asks you to make some changes *before* he directs the other person to make some. In cooperating with him you will most certainly learn valuable lessons in patience, character, and hope (Rom. 5:3-5). You might pray this: "Father, you can see the problem I am facing. I want your solution, whatever it is. Place within my heart your love, for I sense that mine is so inadequate."

Praying for Financial Help. Since God has guaranteed to supply all your needs, you can live above being anxious about insufficient funds. However, before you begin praying about money matters you will have to agree to some conditions which God has set forth in his Word.

First, God is not in the business of supplying your every whim, like a great celestial Santa Claus. He expects you to be a good steward of what you already have. Then, you can trust him for what you still need. Also, he doesn't give to us if we will not work to earn our living (see 2 Thessalonians 3:10).

Second, Malachi 3:10 says that tithing is part of God's divine financial planning program, not only for his work here on earth but also for our own blessing as well.

Third, in Luke 6:38 Jesus says that if you want to receive you have to give to those who are in need. Then "it will be given to you. A good measure, pressed down, shaken together and running over. . . . For with the measure you use, it will be measured to you."

Finally, God wants to become your financial adviser. He wants the opportunity to direct the way you spend your money. His guidance may be rather close and intense until you learn proper procedures for handling your finances. But with God as a financial guide you will always have everything you need.

You might pray thus, "Lord I am having problems financially and want your help in getting things straightened out. I agree to let you lead me so that I use my resources properly. Help me to spend wisely. Lead me so that I will not covet unnecessary things."

Praying For Guidance. To desire God's will in all matters is surely a good thing. It becomes so much easier to do his will when you understand that he does not give direction as a taskmaster would. His guidance is given so that you might avoid pitfalls in life and so that you might extend his kingdom. You need to pray not only for direction but for wisdom as well. At times God will tell you exactly what to do. At other times he wants you to go forward and make your own decisions. It is at such times that you need special wisdom.

When praying for the ability to make good decisions you might say, "Father, teach me wisdom and good judgment. James 1:5 says that you will give me wisdom if I ask for it. I ask for it now. May I be a person who perceives right from wrong and learns always to choose the right. Help me to know your voice and to test carefully all the circumstances so that I do not become deceived. May I learn not to attribute things to you until I am certain they are from you."

Continue to pray frequently for the initial request until the answer comes. You will not need to pray the same prayer all over again, but you need to pray for specific situations concerning the original petition. You will be praying prayers to help the situation on its way to an answer. For instance, after praying for the salvation of a person, you might follow up by praying that God will place Christian people near this person in order to influence him or her.

Remember, since prayer is personal communication with God there can be no set formula for engaging in it. I have made some suggestions that I hope will help. But you must remember the only place you will truly learn to pray is *in prayer*, where God is the teacher.

And, as we further contemplate prayer, this most vital aspect of warfare, we need to consider what Jesus said to Peter in Matthew 26:40 (and what he no doubt directed to the rest of the disciples, including us).

Just prior to the Cross, Jesus went to Gethsemane with a number of disciples to pray. After entering the garden, some disciples knelt to pray while Peter,

James, and John followed Jesus a short distance further before kneeling to pray. Jesus proceeded still further until he was alone. Then he began to pray. Later he returned to the disciples only to find them sleeping. When they awoke, Jesus spoke to them with words that really speak to all of us: "What, could you not watch with Me one hour?" (Matt. 26:40, NKJV).

FINALLY . . .

Are you beginning to see how powerful these unseen enemies are in your life? Do you think you will recognize them whenever they come against you? Do you know where the battlefronts will be?

As I said at the very beginning, after reading all of this you may be tempted to throw up your hands and quit. But don't. Why should Satan be the victor in your life? Jesus said that "the thief [Satan] comes only to steal and kill and destroy; I have come that [you] may have life, and have it to the full" (John 10:10), or as other versions read "have life more abundantly." The quality of your life here on earth depends on your overcoming the "thief" of good living. That should be reason enough to work at this business of overcoming.

Jesus promised his disciples, and us, that "in this world you will have trouble. But take heart! I have overcome the world" (John 16:33). John, in his first epistle, says that because Jesus overcame, we "are from God and have overcome [the spirit of the antichrist] because the one who is in you [Jesus] is greater than the one who is in the world" (1 John 4:4).

Then the Apostle Paul summed up the way to overcome in Romans 12. He urged us to "offer your bodies as living sacrifices, holy and pleasing to God . . . be transformed by the renewing of your mind. . . . Hate what is evil; cling to what is good. . . . Be joyful in hope, patient in affliction, faithful in prayer. . . . Do not be overcome by evil, but overcome evil with good" (Rom. 12:1-2, 9, 12, 21).

What will be the final outcome of our struggle to overcome in this world? "Then I saw a new heaven and a new earth, for the first heaven and the first earth had passed away . . . And I heard a loud voice from the throne saying, 'Now the dwelling of God is with men, and he will live with them. They will be his people, and God himself will be with them and be their God. He will wipe every tear from their eyes. There will be no more death or mourning or crying or pain, for the old order of things has passed away. . . . I am making everything new! . . . he who overcomes will inherit all this, and I will be his God and he will be my son' " (Rev. 21:1, 3, 5, 7).

Brothers and sisters in Christ, I exhort you to overcome!

NOTES

1. James Montgomery, *Prayer Is the Soul's Sincere Desire.*
2. A. W. Tozer, *The Pursuit of God* (Harrisburg, Penn.: Christian Publications, 1982), 49-51.